RECALIBRATE YOUR CHURCH

How Your Church Can Reach Its Full Kingdom Impact

DR. TROY H. JONES

www.recalibrategroup.com

Recalibrate Your Church
Dr. Troy H. Jones
©2016, The Recalibrate Group
www.recalibrategroup.com

ISBN 978-1-5307-3504-4

All Scripture quotations, unless otherwise indicated, are taken from The Holy Bible, *New International Version*®, *NIV*®, Copyright ©1973, 1978, 1984, 2011 by Biblica, Inc.® Used by permission. All rights reserved worldwide.

Printed in the United States

"This is not your typical church growth book; it is a book about your church having a Kingdom impact on your communities and world. I highly recommend this book to any pastor or leader who desires to challenge the status quo and recapture the vision buried deep inside of them."

—Mark Batterson
New York Times Bestselling Author of *The Circle Maker* and Lead Pastor of National Community Church

"Nothing is stronger than culture in your church. Vision, Mission, Core Values, Goals, Strategic Plans and all other important issues are neutralized at best and impotent at worst in an unhealthy toxic culture. In *Recalibrate Your Church*, Dr. Troy Jones gives you not just an understanding of your present challenges, but guides you through nine practices to recalibrate your church and embrace you and your church's destiny."

—Dr. Samuel R. Chand
Leadership Consultant and Author of *Leadership Pain*

"Troy Jones is one of the great visionaries and innovators when it comes to church leadership of our day. Growing out of his own incredible experience, *Recalibrate Your Church* contains insights and principles that I believe can help any church grow and reach its full Kingdom potential in Christ! After reading this book, you won't be able to settle into comfortable complacency. The Holy Spirit will ignite a recalibration revolution."

—Dr. Kent Ingle
President of Southeastern University and Author of *This Adventure Called Life: Discovering Your Divine Design*

"Troy Jones has literally written a manifesto on how existing churches, large and small, can reposition themselves for the future; how they need to regularly recalibrate. If you are looking for another formula book on "how-to" grow the church, *Recalibrate Your Church* is not for you. On the other hand if you are willing to dig deep into the culture of your church and be willing to recalibrate even the person at the top, then I cannot recommend any book higher than this one. Hats off to Troy Jones for helping leaders recalibrate their churches now and for the future."

—Dick Hardy
Founder of The Hardy Group

"In Troy Jones' must-read book, he challenges pastors to take an honest assessment of their churches and to stop defending what isn't working. From church environments to personal planning, his book will help your church go from existing to thriving. God has not given up on your church!"

—Rob Ketterling
Author of *Change Before You Have To* and *Thrill Sequence.*
Founder and Lead Pastor of River Valley Church

"Troy has written a book that not only *motivates* but also *educates* leaders. Every entity must recalibrate in order to function at the highest capacity. However, if one is not equipped with the knowledge, or inspiration to do so, breakdown is inevitable! Troy's work not only gives us the *want to's* but masterfully offers the *how-to.* I would recommend this read for every person charged with the responsibility of navigating ANY organization!"

—Roger Archer
Founder and Lead Pastor of Puyallup Foursquare Church

"Troy Jones is the pastor of New Life Church here in the Pacific Northwest. He has led his church in growing from 1500 to over 3500 in recent years. Troy has a heart to help pastors and churches reach their Kingdom potential. He has a very unique ability to help established churches with a rich history to re-examine themselves, and to get "back on mission." His book "Recalibrate" will be a great help to any church leader seeking to move their church forward. I highly recommend the book to you."

—Dr. Mel Ming
Leadership Development Resources LLC, Founding Partner

"I have known Dr. Troy H Jones for many, many years. His leadership is inspirational and contagious. Troy has a passion for healthy churches and healthy leadership. His attention to detail in this book about vision and keeping the dream alive will make a difference in your thought processes. This is a must read book for a leader who wants to impact the world!"

—Dary R. Northrop
Senior Pastor of Timberline Church

"As the world gets darker the church needs to shine brightly, full of the hope, truth, and the grace that makes a real difference. In *Recalibrate Your Church* Troy shares a practical path that any leader can follow. His message is simple and he shares it in an engaging way. I highly recommend this book!

—Jason Miles
Bestselling Author and Co-founder of Sew Powerful

"Every church needs to recalibrate. Over the years of my leadership I have watched many leaders endeavor to recalibrate their congregations. Many times this ends up with a train wreck. This happens because it is easy to miss some vital principles and practices in leading established churches. Troy outlines in his book well thought out and proven practices for leaders to recalibrate their churches. More than a bunch of philosophy he provides practical steps at the end of each chapter for the leader to recalibrate their leadership and church. God wants your church to reach its full Kingdom impact. I know it is uncomfortable to challenge the status quo, but the future of your church and the people in your community are worth it!"

—Dr. Rick Ross
Senior Pastor of Concord First Assembly

"Through this book Troy will reignite the vision the Holy Spirit placed in your heart for your church and give you the practical narrative to see it become a reality. On a personal level the practical truths found in this book were the catalyst for Canvas Church achieving our vision. It gave us permission to put a "date on the calendar" and get moving."

—Kevin Geer
Lead Pastor of Canvas Church

"I have had the fortune of knowing Dr. Troy Jones since he was a teenager, and have seen him grow in knowledge of the Word and leadership of the church. He has a God-inspired burden for the health of local churches. Having witnessed first-hand, on several occasions, the monumental and positive impact "relaunching" has had on our church, this book has much to offer, and a must-read, for pastors and leaders desiring to break through natural barriers limiting church health, growth and relevancy."

—Dr. John Hoole
Board Member of New Life Church

"Troy is an energetic, tireless, creative leader who simply refuses to settle for the status quo. I have watched Troy and benefited from his practical wisdom for over two decades. In that time I have been impressed with the selfless manner in which he prefers other leaders and pastors with his time, treasure and talent. *Recalibrate* is just one more manifestation of Troy's character. This book is for anyone who refuses to do business as usual. This book is for anyone who has said, 'There must be a better way!' This book is for anyone who has been looking for a man of character and proven leadership excellence to advise and invest in their leadership."

—Bret Allen
Senior Pastor of Bethel Church

"Dr. Troy abounds with the experience of one who has seen much before, but at the same time the enthusiasm of one who knows there still much to discover. In a life, church and world that sees constant shifts and changes, consistent RECALIBRATION is not only an important topic but an essential goal for us all. I'm grateful for this book, his ministry but mostly his example in doing this throughout the years."

—Dan Lian
Speaker and Evangelist

"Recalibrate is strategically written by an outstanding leader who understands church growth. Throughout this book Troy Jones captures the principles that will breathe life into any ministry. Grab a copy for yourself and your team and reignite your church."

—Chris Sonksen
Founder of ChurchBOOM and Lead Pastor of South Hills Church

Dedication

To the congregation and elders of New Life Church: Thank you for your grace in allowing me to lead significant cultural change in our church. In many ways, you were the launch pad for many of these principles and practices outlined in this book. Your example of courage and your willingness to confront the status quo is truly amazing. Jana and I are forever grateful for you! We can't adequately express our love for the whole New Life Family. These last twelve years have been an unbelievable adventure, full of ups and downs. But looking back and seeing the hand of God on our growth and momentum is truly a mark of His grace and favor. Hold on! We have just begun!

Contents

Introduction

My wife and I sat in a restaurant one night with our friends, Stan and Karen Russell. Although Stan has pastored his church for twenty years, I could sense him struggling. He needed to talk, so we listened as Stan openly shared thoughts about his church, including some very honest frustrations.

Although Stan had enjoyed some incredible days in his ministry, his voice revealed some real discouragement and an erosion of personal leadership confidence. After two decades of faithful work, Stan felt that everything at his church had grown stagnant and sluggish. Moreover, the church had stopped growing.

"Stan," I said to him, "the best days for your ministry are before you, not behind you! God put a dream deep inside of your heart. He is going to restore confidence and build momentum in your church."

I let him soak that in, then looked him in the eye and asked, "What is God saying to you? What is God birthing in your heart? What has the Spirit begun to stir inside of you? Let's put a date on it! Let's put a stake in the ground and relaunch your church."

Our conversation sparked something deep inside of Stan—and candidly, inside of me, too. Somehow, this incredible leader had lost all perspective and confidence. I got so angry with the enemy! I've seen this happen time and again.

"Write down what's in your heart," I told Stan. "At this moment, don't let anything be a hurdle in your mind. This is just between you and God."

Then I challenged him: "For a moment, imagine that you've fired yourself as pastor. Now, come back and start all over again. What would you do on your first day at your new church?"

Right on the spot, ideas began to pour out of Stan. He got very animated and began to describe ideas about the Sunday gathering, the staff, and the facilities. I couldn't help but feel like this was a tipping point for Stan's leadership and life.

"You are about to celebrate twenty years at your church," I said. "Let's recalibrate and relaunch your church! Let's pretend this is day one of you pastoring."

Stan did just that. Over the next twelve months, God not only helped his church regain its momentum, but also (and perhaps just as important) helped restore Stan's confidence and enthusiasm. Listen to the excitement in his words: "I regained my confidence as a leader, and we recaptured momentum. With the recaptured momentum and the positive results from the Relaunch Initiative, we have learned to use our leadership muscles. The body has grown stronger as a result."

Stan is one of many leaders who have successfully applied the recalibration principles and practices detailed in this book. Each one has seen God restore confidence, provide strong momentum, and once more make these established churches a dynamic part of their communities and reach their full Kingdom impact. I've seen these principles work with churches of all sizes, both large and small.

Tom Colby has served his West Seattle church for twenty years. He, too, had become discouraged in a stagnated ministry. After recalibrating his church, Tom reports:

> "Just wanted to give you a little update on attendance at Westwood Christian Community. This morning our attendance was 176. Amazing! Both services have increased in attendance. This is a new attendance record for us on

a regular Sunday gathering. Something very exciting is happening at Westwood Christian—you can feel it in the air! We are anxious for our next attendance breakthrough!"

When Andrew Murch arrived to pastor an established church with a rich history, he quickly saw his congregation had lost focus and momentum. After he worked to recalibrate his church, he saw it get back on mission and begin to move forward. Andrew reports:

"We won't slow down. The branding for our Relaunch Initiative, "To Be the Church," is literally written on the wall of our lobby and has become a rallying cry in our local church body. We are moving forward, attempting to tackle even greater financial and visionary plans this year and beyond. This first Relaunch Initiative developed a faith and confidence in our body that has been sorely lacking in the last twenty years. It is a first step. What is ahead is a series of strategic initiatives and catalytic moments that will detonate a gospel-centered movement known as LifePoint Church all throughout Clark County."

Each of these stories reflects the heart of this book. You may be a pastor, associate, board member, or influencer in your church. I wrote this book for you. I truly believe in you and what God wants to do in your church.

For the Naysayers

You don't need someone to tell you that the North American church looks more like Rip Van Winkle than it does Captain America. Of the 350,000 churches in North America, 80 percent have either plateaued or are declining.

But I doubt that such dismal stats are haunting you. What eats at you is your own ministry environment. Whenever you take an honest look at a typical Sunday morning, you know something has gone very wrong. It troubles you that you can't put your finger on the problem, much less any tangible solutions. You want answers that will help your church move forward and win people to Christ.

Oh, I know that many naysayers have given up on the local church. They've even pronounced it dead. I think they are both 100 percent right and 100 percent wrong.

They're right in the sense that a great many churches have plateaued or have entered a long, painful era of decline. But they're wrong in the sense that they have overlooked the most important fact: *God has not given up on established churches with a rich history!* He knows they all have stories that need to be recaptured and recalibrated, and He's looking for courageous leaders to step up and lead.

Setting Expectations

Before we go any further, allow me to set a few expectations for this book. This book will NOT:

Tell you how to do church. This book will teach you how to create a culture of continuous recalibration, always taking into consideration its own defining characteristics, character, and calling. It will not emphasize any particular church model. I assume that God has called you to be where you are, and that the Spirit already has started to birth something unique deep within you. While some of my own church models and philosophies will become obvious, I want you to be a leader who hears from God, not a parrot who mimics someone else.

Offer quick fixes. I can already hear some critics: "We don't need *another* book on church revitalization and growth!" And on one level, I agree with them. We certainly do not need a quick-fix, write-out-your-mission-statement-and-core-values book and then watch your church magically grow and get written up in the next church magazine. So let me emphasize this up front: if you recalibrate your church one time, you will get some good results, perhaps even immediate ones. But if that's all you do, you'll wind up with nothing more than a quick fix.

Promise you, "This will be easy!" Recalibrating an established church is painful work. It's never easy. Almost certainly you will lose people. You will have sleepless nights. You will make mistakes. Honestly, if it weren't for the words of Jesus to "go and make disciples," I would recommend taking the easy road and letting your people stay comfortable. Recalibrating is not for the faint of heart!

On the other hand, this book WILL:

Stretch you to dream again for your church. God has birthed a dream inside of your heart. But because you've had some misfires and setbacks, you may have, in effect, thrown in the towel. You're just waiting it out. It's time for you to put on your "big boy pants" and start leading your church!

Reignite a deep love for your church again! You may not even like your church or your own preaching. Honestly, deep down, you would do something else with your life if you had either the money or the opportunity. Stop flirting with the idea of leaving! Either find the courage to recalibrate your church or the grace to resign, but don't merely toy with the idea. Yes, your church has problems. No perfect church exists, any more than a perfect bride exists. My burden for you is that you will so radically recalibrate your own passion for what's happening at your church that you actually start inviting people to come!

Develop your leadership muscles. At the heart of this book lies my desire that you develop new leadership muscles that will recalibrate your own leadership. Many church growth books offer ideas and programs to grow a church, but this book offers principles and practices that will grow you and build "leader muscle mass" deep within you.

Compare it to lifting weights. If a trainer told me, "Troy, get down here and bench press three hundred pounds," I already know the outcome. No matter how much time I had, how much money you gave me, how much coaching you provided, how hard I prayed, how many great ideas you came up with, or how loudly you shouted encouragement to me, I still couldn't bench press three hundred pounds. There's only one way I could bench press so much weight, and that's if I trained to build more muscle. The same is true in your church.

Transform your culture. I wrote this book to help spark cultural change in the church, not programmatic change. The most difficult part of recalibrating an established church is realigning its culture. We will do the hard and complicated work in this book. Far too often, leaders think that if they just craft a mission statement, add a cool service, and start serving coffee, their church will grow. If only it were that easy!

Who's the Audience?

Who did I have in mind when I wrote this book? Who can most benefit from the principles it lays out? I have several audiences in mind:

Lead pastors of established churches. Most of today's books and conferences about church leadership are taught by founding pastors. These pastors have incredible content to offer—but leading a church that you've planted is fundamentally different from leading an established church. The two may look the same to the naked eye, but they differ in crucial ways.

Just think of the differences between remodeling an old house and building a new one. Remodeling requires you to find the load bearing walls, identify any possible leaks, investigate foundational integrity, and discover all the nuances of that old house. New home construction has a very different set of concerns. This book doesn't so much give you a blueprint for planting a new church as it offers sound principles and practices for recalibrating an established one.

All influencers and leaders within a local church. Recalibration concerns all church leaders, whether board members, pastoral staff, small group leaders, children's pastors, youth pastors, associate pastors, volunteers, or any other significant influencers in the church. If you are on staff, know that these principles will also apply to your specific ministry. Even though I won't talk much about departmental recalibration, the principles developed in this book apply equally to every department within a local church.

Business or visionary leaders. Any business could greatly benefit from applying the principles in this book. While I won't refer to many examples from the business world—my chief concern, after all, is the church—I've seen the principles work remarkably well in any number of organizations and businesses.

Let's Get Started

I am praying that God will give you the courage to take an honest look at your church and leadership. It is time to challenge the status quo in your church, business, personal ministries, and even your own life!

I am praying your church would reach its full Kingdom impact. Recalibrating your church is not about making a name for yourself, building the biggest and coolest congregation, or even finding a way to pay the bills. This is not about building your kingdom, but God's. If you care about nothing more than additional bodies, bigger buildings, and larger budgets, then honestly, this book will let you down.

In the next few pages, let me become your personal coach. Allow me to help you create a continuous culture of recalibration in your church and discover the vision deeply embedded inside of your heart!

If you are an emerging leader and have felt skeptical of established churches, I pray God would give you a deep burden for the established church in North America. Or perhaps you are in the last season of your ministry and wondering if you should coast or even try to generate any kind of significant change. I pray God would use the words you're about to read to strike a deep chord in your life.

God wants you to leave a legacy of both courage and momentum. He has no interest in you sitting back, waiting for retirement, or just hanging on until the end. You have the opportunity to lay the groundwork of innovative change for the next generation.

The greatest Kingdom potential in North America lies in recalibrating established churches rich in the kind of redemptive stories that need to be recaptured and rewritten.

You really can do this. So let's get started!

Prologue

THIS OLD HOUSE

I live in an old home with a lot of history behind it, built way back in 1896. Twenty years ago, I saved this house from demolition.

I love my old house. It has an amazing history. Back in the early twentieth century, it was known as the Mercer House. Mr. Thomas Mercer, a Seattle pioneer, bought the land on which his sons built the house. This house served as the first post office for the city of Renton. The house has a history as rich and colorful as that of the Pacific Northwest itself.

Over the years, I have totally remodeled, restructured, and redone every aspect of this house. I built a new foundation. Rewired it. Redid the plumbing. Put on a new roof. Took down some walls and put up new ones. Painted it and installed new floors and carpeting. Today, the house has all the character of a home built in 1896, but all the comfort and quality of a modern home.

Why is the house such an incredible place to live? I was willing to pay the price to remodel it. Remodeling takes work and is very messy. It always costs more than you think and takes longer than you plan. It would have been easier and probably cheaper to buy a newly constructed home. But I couldn't buy a house like that. I wanted the history and legacy of an historic home.

As great as a newly built home is, it doesn't have the character of an old home. There is something beautiful about a home from 1896, and older homes tend to be built better than homes today. (Many contractors have told me that the quality of wood and nails in my house simply don't exist anymore.) Old homes have a character and legacy that make them worth saving—worth paying the price to remodel.

In the same way, I believe established churches are worth saving. There is nothing like an established church that has recovered its Kingdom impact. It has character. Each established church has a great story that needs to be recaptured and rewritten.

Your church is worth remodeling. It is worth stripping down to the rafters of your mission and the foundation of the gospel. It is worth carefully and respectfully discovering what is destroying its value and making it uninhabitable. It is worth preserving, improving, and updating.

Pastor, I believe that the prophet Amos has a word for you. God calls you to "restore the former glory of the house" (Amos 9:11). Yes, *you*. The greatest Kingdom impact in North America lies in recalibrating established churches.

In Scripture, we see God repeatedly recalibrating His people. He wants to do it again, in our day. In appendix A, I have provided a sheet that outlines how God recalibrates His people, from Genesis to Revelation, including a brief discussion of historical context. I am praying He will do it one more time, this time with you!

Recalibrating your church is not some passive, sit-back-and-just-see-what-happens kind of process. You have to *start* again. You have to *dream* again! You have to courageously step up and lead your church.

I pray that as you read this book, God would light a fire of passion in your heart. It is time to dream for your church again! God has placed a dream deep inside of your heart

Part One

THE CULTURE OF RECALIBRATION

Every congregation has a church culture. Your culture includes what you celebrate, the words you use, your traditions—essentially, how you do church. Your church has a distinct culture. My church has one. It can't be seen by the naked eye, but every person who walks through your doors feels it. Your culture is always working in the backdrop of your church; it determines how your people treat each other, respond to change, and envision your church's future.

At times, that culture will become slow and stagnate. You might cover it up. You might pretend it's not happening, but the reality is this: every church culture will face a slow drift.

What does a church do about this natural tendency to drift off mission? What does a church do when its culture becomes sluggish? There are 350,000 churches in North America. Eighty percent of them have plateaued or are in decline. Is there any hope? Is the only answer to sit idly by and watch these churches die a slow death?

> **You cannot effectively lead a church if you suffer from a dry soul.**

I will offer one overall transferable principle in this book that will change everything for you and your church. When I say everything, be forewarned: I literally mean *everything!*

It is not a program or a new church growth idea. Recalibration is a deep philosophy about leadership and the very nature of church life. It will permeate your entire ministry and organization.

Before we start this adventure together, allow me to disclose a few of my own assumptions about you. If these are not true of you, then this book may not help you much.

You passionately love Jesus. This is not a game. You *cannot* effectively lead a church if you suffer from a dry soul. Before you can recalibrate your church, you must recalibrate your own spiritual fervor before God. In the final chapter, I talk about recalibrating your own soul. You may first want to read chapter 14, "Recalibrate Your Soul," if you find yourself spiritually dry.

You are treating your church like an owner, not a renter. Whenever I begin coaching a leader, I always ask this question: "Are you treating your church like an owner or a renter?" There is a big difference. Have you taken ownership of your God-given role at your church? If you are not called and committed to the local body you currently serve, then do yourself and everyone else a favor: get a paying job somewhere else and volunteer at another church. I don't mean this in a cruel way, but the Great Commission is too important for you to waste your church's time and money.

You are ready to stretch your leadership muscles. If you have no interest in learning and stretching yourself, then put down this book right now. I've written it for those eager to address the personal leadership muscles in their lives and ministries. If you get hypersensitive every time someone questions your preaching, ministry model, or philosophy, then you need a "Come to Jesus" meeting with yourself.

But if you long to move your church's mission forward, take ownership and responsibility for the Kingdom impact of your church, and are willing to build leadership muscles in ways that will make you feel uncomfortable—then keep reading.

1

CREATING A CULTURE OF RECALIBRATION

Every moment of change starts with a catalyst, a single event, a question, a moment, or an exchange that causes us to reexamine our current reality and begin to ask deeper, better questions. That moment came for me in the spring of 2010.

I was enjoying a pleasant and encouraging conversation with my friend and mentor, Dr. Alan Johnson. Alan was there the day I gave my life to Christ and has remained alongside me throughout my spiritual journey. His counsel and advice have proven invaluable throughout my life.

We were discussing the recent growth of the church I pastor, New Life Church, and the condition and future of North American churches in general. Alan looked at me and asked, "What transferable principles are you learning that can help leaders? Our churches are in trouble. *Something* is happening at New Life that you need to figure out so you can explain it to other leaders." Although Alan's question struck a chord in my life, something deep and resonant, I had no immediate answer for him.

"What is happening at New Life is bigger than a new building, cool services, and paint on the walls," Alan continued. "You need to do the diligent work required to unearth significant principles that are easily transferable to other leaders."

About the same time, another dear friend and hero of mine, Dr. Mel Ming, told me, "You know intuitively how to lead your church, but that won't help other leaders. You need to develop practical principles and practices that will help other leaders reinvigorate their churches."

God used these men to light a fire in my heart for established churches across North America. Their challenge prompted me to go beyond my own experience at New Life; their words drove me to embed this investigation in rigorous academic study with the goal of making the ideas applicable to other churches.

In response, I started a program of doctoral study in the fall of 2010. I dedicated the next five years of my life to identifying and honing a few transferable principles and practices that could help embolden and encourage leaders of established churches. This single challenge, expressed by both Dr. Johnson and Dr. Ming, led me on a quest for answers and ultimately defined my heartbeat for the established church in North America.

The One Transferable Principle

After analyzing New Life Church's growth, spending five years on doctoral work, working with established churches of all sizes, styles, structures and philosophical approaches and coaching many leaders, I have formulated one core transferable principle about churches and organizations of all sizes and styles: *You either create a culture of continuous recalibration, or your church will slowly and steadily drift off mission.* Period!

In other words, you either recalibrate, or your church will eventually stagnate. This single transferable principle explains why so many churches have stopped growing.

Many churches haven't restarted, rebooted, or relaunched anything new for years, even decades. If you don't intentionally recalibrate your church, then you are choosing to sit idle, lethargically watching while your church eventually drifts into an ingrown, irrelevant, comatose state.

So what does it mean to recalibrate your church? To calibrate means "to plan or devise (something) carefully so as to have a precise use, application, appeal, etc."[1] When things are not calibrated, they work inefficiently, burn through resources, and eventually break down. Churches require precision and care in order to stay on course and avoid mission drift. Established churches need to recalibrate so they can function precisely and effectively in their communities and appeal to the authentic needs of a changing culture, thus fulfilling the great mission of Christ.

> You either create a culture of continuous recalibration, or your church will slowly and steadily drift off mission.

All churches, organizations, and leaders need to recalibrate. It is not a matter of if you need to recalibrate, but when you will need to recalibrate.

It doesn't matter if your church is:

- Missional or attractional
- Big or small
- Urban, suburban, or rural
- Progressive or conservative
- Loud, with contemporary worship, or softer, with liturgical worship

Regardless of your style, shape, size, experience, history, staff, or congregational affiliation, one thing is true about your church: if you don't recalibrate, your congregation will slowly and steadily drift off its mission and die a slow death.

This should *surprise* none of us, because everything in this world needs to be periodically recalibrated. Think about it:

- Your body shuts down every night and wakes up every morning.
- When your computer gets slow, the experts tell you to reboot it—shut it down and restart it.
- When your Wi-Fi stops working, you call your Internet provider, who tells you to reset your modem.
- When the scale gives you an unfavorable number, you kick it, hoping to get a new number more to your liking.

Recalibrating is something more than a practice, an event, or a moment. It is a perspective and a way of viewing your entire ministry and organization. It becomes a cultural norm, a way to approach every aspect of leadership and church life.

The theory of the bell curve states that every organization will hit its peak, at which time it must either reinvent itself or go backward. Every successful leader knows this intuitively. So you often see signs that say, "Grand Opening," or "Under New Management." It's why Apple always seems to be releasing new versions of its iPhone or iPad. When you infuse a culture of recalibration into your church, you make sure that your church will never hit the peak of the bell curve and then begin to drift inexorably downward. This one practice allows you to get ahead of the bell curve.

How Often Do I Need to Recalibrate?

Church leaders tend to want to find the latest silver bullet or hit program they need to grow their churches. We all want to add the latest piece of software . . . but few of us want to update the church's cultural operating systems. This comes to the forefront in one of the first questions leaders often ask me: "How often do I need to recalibrate?" While nothing is wrong with this question, let me assure you, it's not that easy!

The real challenge is to create a *culture* of recalibration. You must create a culture of recalibration that becomes an integral part of the life and bloodstream of your church, a culture where change becomes normal and not a process that puts the church into a tailspin. To recalibrate effectively, you have to infuse new principles into your congregation and build new leadership muscles in your own life.

When leaders ask how often they need to recalibrate, it reveals that they tend to create events and programs, rather than creating a culture that transforms every spectrum and facet of the organization. The real goal, therefore, is to create a culture of recalibration, not merely a series of cosmetic changes. The goal is to create a new cultural norm, not a pile of hype that will get you some quick results but more than likely frustrate a lot of people.

A culture of recalibration will manifest in two very specific cycles:

1. Cultural, holistic recalibration (every 3 to 5 years)

Cultural recalibration refers to an evaluation of the whole instead of a separation into parts. Cultural recalibration is holistic by its very nature. It involves a thorough reexamination of the entire ministry from the ground up. Rather than shuffling a few chairs and painting a few walls, cultural recalibration means scrutinizing every aspect of the organization. Because the changes are often seismic, cultural recalibration should occur in a cycle of every three to five years.

Cultural recalibration addresses the cultural operating systems of the organization, including its biblical mission, core values, and cultural language. When you undertake a cultural, holistic recalibration, you are, in effect, relaunching your church.

Cultural recalibration begins with a distinctive question that will turn your congregation upside down. The same question did that very thing at Intel, the world's largest computer chip maker. Under the leadership of Andrew S. Grove, Intel has also become one of the most admired companies on the planet. In his book *Only the Paranoid Survive,* Grove recalls a story about being in the office with

Intel's chairman and CEO, Gordon Moore. The pair was discussing the future of their company. In the middle of their conversation, Grove looked at Moore and said, "If we got kicked out and the board brought in a new CEO, what do you think he would do?" After a short pause for honest reflection, Grove finished his own question: "Why shouldn't you and I walk out the door, come back in, and do it ourselves?"[2]

All leaders need to personalize this question. Andy Stanley personalized it for pastors when he wrote, "If we all got kicked off the staff and the board, and an outside group (a group of leaders who were fearlessly committed to the mission of this church) took our place, what changes would they introduce?"[3] Every leader needs to wrestle with this question, especially pastors trying to lead a cultural recalibration.

Fire yourself, pastor, before someone else does it for you! Metaphorically, cultural recalibration means fire yourself, walk out the door, return, and start over. If you were to restart your church today, moving into the neighborhood with fresh energy and vision, what would you do to reach your community for Jesus? This one question will mess you up and change everything.

My research indicates that all organizations need to have a cultural, holistic recalibration every three to five years. Additionally, my personal study of the ninety year history of the church I pastor clearly shows it. In Appendix B, I include "Recalibration for New Life Church: 2003-2016," a document that highlights the major moments of recalibration for New Life from 2003 to 2016.

2. Continuous, specific recalibration (all the time)

Whenever someone asks me, "How often do I need to recalibrate?" I always reply, "All the time!" I like the word "continuous"— never stopping, without interruption, unceasing, and ongoing. Continuous recalibration must happen all the time.

Continuous recalibration refers to significant adjustments and improvements to specific ministries, practices, and systems within the church. In chapter 13, I discuss in detail the concept of continuous improvements and how this one leadership practice will transform everything in your congregation.

Leaders also frequently ask me, "Does everything need to change at my church?" The answer is no. But everything does *eventually* need to be recalibrated. We tend to think every program is either bad or good, and therefore needs either to be tossed or kept. Not true. All programs and systems need to be recalibrated, while many need a graceful funeral. I guarantee, however, that ALL programs and systems, at some point, need to be recalibrated, both in the heart of the leadership and in the congregation.

The following diagram should help you to grasp the main differences between cultural recalibration and continuous recalibration.

Cultural Recalibration	Continuous Recalibration
➤ Every 3 to 5 years	➤ All the time
➤ Holistic	➤ Specific
➤ Relaunches the church	➤ Fine-tunes the church
➤ Transforms the culture	➤ Cultivates the culture
➤ Rethinks everything	➤ Rethinks a few things
➤ Mission critical	➤ Mission critical
➤ Holistic systems & practices	➤ Specific systems
➤ Catalyst for innovation	➤ Catalyst for progress
➤ Involves everyone	➤ Involves key leaders

Churches Already Recalibrate

Most churches and organizations can point to key recalibration moments in their history. In fact, in recalibrating a church, it is essential to learn these moments of recalibration and recapture the story of these significant moments in the life of the church.

Consider several times when a church tends to recalibrate:

- A new pastor
- A move into a new facility
- Some unexpected tragedy or crisis in the church starts a chain reaction that prompts a season of recalibration
- Finances drop so low the church has no choice but to recalibrate
- A church split causes a chain reaction of recalibration

But do you see a possible problem here? Every established church eventually runs into a dilemma: at some point, you will have to *intentionally* recalibrate because the natural times won't exist. Established churches that don't intentionally recalibrate get entrenched, because eventually the opportunities to recalibrate will diminish. You can be the new pastor only once. You can't keep building new buildings.

You hope tragedies don't strike regularly. Therefore:

- You have to create chaos when there is no chaos.
- You have to create tension where there is no tension.
- You have to lead when people would rather remain comfortable.

In other words, you have to intentionally recalibrate your congregation, aside from the honeymoon periods, building of new facilities, new staff hires, or tragedies.

During my doctoral study, I read all the board minutes and annual business meetings of New Life Church, from 1926 to the present.

I also interviewed people who were around during the formative days of Renton Assembly (the former name of the church). As I read and re-read the minutes of every board meeting, interviewed key people, and judiciously studied the history of New Life, I determined one constant: *Every time* the church recalibrated and started new ministries, it grew and reached new people. And *every time* the church stopped dreaming and creating, it suffered a period of strife and decline. I observed that rough patches occurred only when the church stopped dreaming, creating, and recalibrating its vision.

One of the roughest periods came in 1949, when the church split. A new pastor had arrived in 1946, and from 1946–1949, the minutes revealed very little innovation. The church became stagnated and started to grow inward. This led to difficult times for both the pastor and the congregation: disagreements about styles, fashions, ministries and other side issues contributed to a loss of confidence in that pastor, resulting in an ugly split. Fortunately, Renton Assembly recalibrated again under new leadership in 1950, and as a result, got back on mission.

> Established churches that don't intentionally recalibrate get entrenched, because eventually the opportunities to recalibrate will diminish.

What is God Birthing in Your Heart?

I always ask the same first question of every frustrated church leader who tells me he has reached the end of his rope: "What is God birthing in your heart?" I do not ask, "How can you grow your church?" or "How can you reach young families?" or "How can you imitate some contemporary church across the country that you're aware of only through blogs and Instagram?"

Church leaders *have to know* they have heard from God. Church leaders need to know they have providential direction and divine assignment from heaven. Recalibrating is all about discovering what God is doing in your church and joining with Him in doing it. It's not about doing a bunch of cool things to boost lagging attendance.

What is God birthing deep down in your soul? There is a dream inside of you! If you are called by God, He has planted this dream in your heart already.

God creates momentum; we merely cultivate it.

I pray that God would use this book to awaken that dream. It may be buried, it may need dusting off, it may be sleeping; however, I believe God put a vision inside of you that only you can accomplish. Perhaps it has been derailed for years, leaving you discouraged and feeling paralyzed. No doubt it will take leadership confidence and courage to unearth the vision inside of you and then to act on it.

Once you get laser-beam clarity about what God is speaking to you, then you have to hit the tarmac and lead your church with courage and confidence. Hitting the tarmac requires leaders to date it, define it, and do it. In chapter 3, I will discuss the significance of hitting the tarmac, while in chapter 12, I will provide you with practical ways to date it, define it, and do it.

Momentum changes everything. When you have it, you look better than you are; when you don't, you look worse than you are. We need to recognize, however, that we cannot and do not create momentum. God creates momentum; we merely cultivate it. It is God who sends us waves of momentum. You and I need to learn the appropriate principles and practices that enable us to cultivate the momentum God gives us, but we do not create it. You must discern and discover what God already is doing within your congregation, and then cultivate that momentum by learning the skills and practices it takes to ride that wave.

Think about a surfer. Surfers don't create waves; they ride waves. They learn skills and practices to effectively catch good waves. If they don't, the wave will crush them.

Far too often, leaders think in terms of "hype" rather than God-sent momentum. Hype is man-made and has no lasting substance. Divine momentum, however, is God-inspired and will transform a church. While I am not totally against hype, I have learned that at the end of the day, it leaves people disillusioned and produces no lasting results.

People in the business world often ask me, "Do business leaders need to ask the same question?" Although this isn't a book about business, my answer is, "Yes." We *all* have to know God is birthing something deep inside of us. Call it a moral compass or leadership imperative, label it as insight or intuition, but whatever you call it, this providential assignment and clear, divine direction provides you with the organizational clarity and spiritual vitality you need to march forward with confidence and vision.

In his book *Courageous Leadership,* Bill Hybels expresses the personal urgency of understanding such a divine vision: "If God has given you a kingdom vision, if you see it clearly and feel it deeply, you had better take responsibility for it. You had better give your life to it. That's why God made you a leader. That's your unique calling. That's what you and I will be held accountable for someday."[4] You have to lead with spiritual authority and *know,* deep down inside, that you have heard from God.

You are about to embark on an adventure full of ups and downs. Instead of making a few plans and hoping God will bless them, you need to do the hard work of discovering what God already wants to bless. You'll need 100 percent confidence that the changes you feel stirring in your heart are from God, not from the hyped program in the latest book you read, a church gimmick, or some idea that you found on Google. People will resist or even reject your ideas if they lack full confidence that you have heard from God.

This is the pivotal question of recalibration. The question is not about growing your church, making a fancy name for yourself, showing off at your denomination's next event, or anything else. It is about one thing: what is God stirring in your heart, deep down inside of you? Recalibration is about your church reaching its full Kingdom impact, not about building your own little kingdom to receive some kind of meaningless applause from your fellow pastor friends.

Catalytic Moments Where Everything Changes

Moments take place in the life of a leader and organization where everything changes. These moments may be obvious to everyone or evident only to the eyes of the leader or a few key people. I refer to these times as "catalytic moments."

Recalibration is about identifying those catalytic moments. In chemistry, a catalyst speeds up the rate and power of a chemical reaction. A reaction that otherwise could take days or even years gets sped up by the introduction of a new element. Once that new element gets introduced, the reaction just takes off. You could say that the catalyst creates chemical momentum. Your role as a visionary leader is to discern and cultivate those catalytic moments in your church and then maximize the momentum that God sends.

In his book *The Tipping Point: How Little Things Can Make a Big Difference,* Malcolm Gladwell introduces the concept of "tipping points."[5] He discusses dramatic moments, or tipping points, where everything can change in almost the blink of an eye. He defines a tipping point as "the moment of critical mass, the threshold, the boiling point."[6] Tipping points are moments of great sensitivity.

Think of recalibration not in terms of a program or campaign, but in terms of identifying the providential tipping points for your church. Think of it like a divine catalyst. There will come a moment of great significance when your preparation aligns with God's providence. The leadership practices you learn in this book will allow you to ride the crest of that outpouring to experience your full Kingdom impact in your community and the world.

Let's Start a Recalibrate Revolution

I believe with all my heart that the greatest Kingdom potential we have in North America lies in recalibrating established churches with a rich history but that have slowly and steadily drifted off mission.

I know many church leaders have given up on the local church. They are wrong! While I believe we need to plant churches, we grossly miss our greatest opportunity by sitting idle as we watch 80 percent of our 350,000 churches plateau or decline.

I don't mean to sound harsh or unkind, but brace yourself for my next comment. I mean it in the most redemptive way possible: *Recalibrate or resign!* Do yourself, your spouse, your elders, and your church a favor. Either find the courage to recalibrate, or find the grace to resign.

I know it takes great courage for a leader to either recalibrate or resign. The far easier thing is to do nothing. But it is time to start a Recalibrate Revolution! This takes bold and clear leadership and a rousing call to action. America needs the Church to wake up and become obsessed with the Great Commission.

Either find the courage to recalibrate, or find the grace to resign.

I worked with one leader who said he wanted to recalibrate his church; he resigned three months later. "I recalibrated my life," he told me in a phone conversation. "Thank you!" He left to lead another church.

I confess that I didn't have *that* particular outcome in mind! But this leader discovered that the only way for him to personally recalibrate was to resign. I deeply respect him for this, because I know it took great courage. I believe the Kingdom of God is stronger today because this leader had the courage to resign, instead of continuing the unsatisfying status quo and watching his church slowly die.

Many individuals have a negative opinion of short-tenured pastors. I used to share that viewpoint, but over the years, I've changed my opinion. I now believe that some leaders simply can't or are unwilling to recalibrate their leadership in their current ministry environment. They would be better off, therefore, leading a church for three to five years and then leaving to serve another congregation. The very act of transition prompts both leaders and churches to recalibrate.

It is time for a Recalibrate Revolution—an urgent call for churches to challenge the status quo, refuse to accept that they are slowly dying, and redeem the history and stories of their churches.

What would happen, I wonder, if every established church and church leader in North America would:

- Have enough courage to rethink everything? *Really.* No sacred cows. No personal agendas. EVERYTHING!
- Pause long enough to make sure the Great Commission still burns deeply in the hearts of the church? Not just on some forgotten wall somewhere.
- Metaphorically walk out of the office, fire themselves, and start again? Day one all over again!
- Totally depend on God for dreams bigger than any one leader?
- Have a clear and compelling vision for the church?
- Step out in faith and trust God for results?

A Recalibrate Revolution may or may not be possible. Perhaps we can't recalibrate all 350,000 churches in America. But we can start with one . . . your church.

Coaching Assignments

1. Read or research the history of your church. At what natural times in the life of your church has it recalibrated? Describe any periods when the church drifted from its mission and vision. What does this teach you about your church?

2. Honestly answer this question: "What is God birthing deep down in your soul?" Get away for a day or two. Grab a pad of paper. Wrestle with this question. Write down your responses.

3. Speaking metaphorically, what changes would you make if you "fired" yourself and then re-hired yourself as the new pastor?

2

THE FLASHING RED LIGHT
ON YOUR DASHBOARD

I could feel the tension building as I coached a pastor over the phone. I could tell he wanted to ask me something, but didn't exactly know how to word his question. Finally, exasperated, he just blurted it out: "Why do you want your church to grow?"

Then he admitted, "Sometimes I am not sure if my motives are about people coming to Jesus or me wanting a bigger church. Do I want to grow the church to look better, or do I really want to reach people? Do I want my name to be in some church growth magazine, or really impact people for Christ?"

Undoubtedly, his comments came laced with sarcasm and years of tiresome lectures about church growth. But I have to confess that his honesty and vulnerability felt refreshing.

All of us, at one time or another, have thrown out well-meaning excuses:

"I am not about numbers."

"I am a faithful servant."

"Success is dangerous . . . not good for the ego."

"We may not be growing numerically, but we're growing deep."

But let's be honest—many times, these are just excuses that help us sleep better at night, while covering up the lack of vision and leadership in our churches.

After letting my friend vent for a bit, I replied, "If you have a problem with your personal ego and arrogance, I get it. All of us need to deal with our ego and pride. The very fact you are willing to admit this shows me something very healthy about your soul. But don't let this stop you from moving your church forward! Here is what I know: your church needs to wake up and reach its full Kingdom impact for your community and the world. You are ignoring some obvious warning signs in your church, and it is time for you to step up and lead."

Would your community care, or even notice, if the church shut down today?

I then asked several probing questions:

"Is your church achieving its full Kingdom impact right now in your community?"

"Would your community care, or even notice, if the church shut down today?"

"Are you personally excited to show up every Sunday?"

"What is God birthing in your heart?"

The pastor remained silent. But very clearly, he knew something was wrong. As he stared at the dashboard of his church, he could see the warning lights flashing.

No doubt all of us have to deal with our own egos in regard to numbers and why we want to see our churches move forward. I wouldn't be honest if I suggested my own ego doesn't factor into the equation. But all of us need to surrender our egos at the foot of the cross. This is about God's Kingdom, not yours or mine!

Don't compromise the future of your church just because you fear a potential ego problem. The bottom line is that your community desperately needs a thriving church, not a mediocre or dying one. It needs a church that's alive, filled with vision, and impacting people with the redemptive message of Christ.

That flashing red light is trying to say to you, "If you don't stop and deal immediately with this issue, then get ready for a breakdown. Your church has begun a slow and steady mission drift." Stop ignoring the flashing red light on your church's dashboard! The future of your church is at stake.

Deceptively Healthy Churches

One of the most common reasons that leaders either ignore or don't see the flashing red light is that their churches become "deceptively healthy." By most measures, our congregations appear strong on the outside, but if the truth were known, we'd see clear signs of decay and disease. It's as though a massive aneurysm ready to burst lies in the center of the church's brain—undetected but deadly.

Deceptively healthy churches have slowly and steadily drifted off mission, and either no one notices or no one will willingly admit it. By all "normal" standards, we may appear healthy: Attendance is fine. Finances are okay. Building remains standing. Christians are still showing up.

But deep down, the leader knows that all of these things merely mask the reality that the church has wandered off mission. Something feels "off." There is activity but little progress. There is effort but no energy.

Studies vary on how many deceptively healthy churches we have in America. Thom Rainer estimates that of the 350,000 churches in our country, 40 percent have symptoms of sickness, and another 40 percent are very sick. This means that 80 percent of our churches are deceptively healthy or just downright unhealthy. Like Typhoid Mary, they walk around full of disease and sickness, yet never show a sign. They live on the outside while dying on the inside.

Deceptively healthy churches catch a virus I call "mission drift,"[7] which has reached epidemic proportions. Over a period of time, our churches have centered on everything but the Great Commission.

We fight over worship style. We prop up outdated programs. We focus on minor or obscure doctrinal issues that divide the church. Many churches have become more passionate about the volume of the music or a favorite ministry program than about reaching lost neighbors.

Every church has some form or degree of mission drift. It's not a question of if, but when you'll start to slowly drift off mission. The longer your church's history, the more likely this virus will destroy the life and emotional energy of your congregation. Unless you act with ruthless intentionality, this virus will continue to spread, causing an epidemic throughout your church.

Established churches do not drift off mission overnight; it happens gradually. Peter Greer and Chris Horst wrote their insightful book *Mission Drift* for leaders, charities, and churches. Through their extensive research, they have concluded that every organization inevitably will drift from its founding mission. "It's that simple. It will happen. Slowly, silently, and with little fanfare, organizations routinely drift from their original purpose, and most will never return to their original intent. It has happened repeatedly throughout history and it was happening to us."[8]

Deceptively healthy churches measure church health by bodies, budgets, and buildings, and not by spiritual transformation. Healthy churches go much deeper than this and measure the church by the Great Commission and deep, cultural "whys." Jesus gave His Church the "why," often referred to as the Great Commission. But one could easily call it, "The Great Why." Truly healthy churches keep the Great Commission at the center of their ministries.

Deceptively healthy churches may have a veneer of success—a very impressive, very beautiful, even very enticing veneer—but something other than Matthew 28 lies at the core. Our mission is to make disciples of all nations (Matthew 28:19) and mirror the redemptive life of Christ who came to "seek and to save the lost" (Luke 19:10). Understanding the mission (the "why") instills in a congregation and its leaders a deep conviction more potent than any great idea or technique. Until leaders ignite a passion for the mission of their church, all strategies become merely like the latest church growth fad—temporary and ultimately meaningless.

You can ignore the flashing red light on your church's dashboard, but you can't avoid the problems it's trying to bring to your attention. The light is trying to warn you that something is wrong and that you have become deceptively healthy.

> **Many church leaders face a gradual erosion of personal leadership confidence.**

I have identified seven flashing red lights that indicate your church is either deceptively healthy or just about to break down. These red lights clearly indicate that the time has come to recalibrate your church.

1. Erosion of leadership confidence

One reason why leaders don't recalibrate their churches is that they have lost their own personal leadership confidence. They have tried something like this recalibration stuff before. This is one red light they would never admit out loud.

Many church leaders face a gradual erosion of personal leadership confidence. Even reading a book makes them cringe. They say things like:

"I am not sure this can be done."

"I have tried this before."

"I am not sure I can do this."

I have met many church leaders who feel, after decades of ministry, that they no longer feel relevant, or they simply can't keep up with the current speed of change. This issue is very hard to identify and openly admit, but if church leaders were honest, they'd agree they've lost their personal leadership confidence.

Leaders can have all the courage in the world, but if they lack confidence, they will paralyze themselves with emotional talk and therefore take no action. Even courageous leaders may find themselves stagnated and unable to move forward, because they lack leadership confidence.

My doctoral recalibration research and project involved seven leaders, all from churches that needed recalibration. On January 27, 2014, God brought together these seven leaders to lead their churches toward a catalytic change.

- These pastors had an average tenure of ten years. Three had seventeen or more years at their churches; four had four years or less.
- These seven churches represented 405 years of history combined. The average age of the churches: Fifty-eight years.
- The average age of the pastors was forty-four. Three of them were under thirty-six, and four were older than forty-five.
- Three churches were located in cities/towns of more than 91,000 people; four were in communities under 66,000.

For nine months, I coached each of these leaders through the three phases of recalibrating their churches, helping each one develop their own Relaunch Initiative. As part of my research, I carefully performed a quantitative and qualitative study that included both pre-testing and post-testing. My findings amazed us all.

The one that most surprised me, by far, was the issue of personal leadership confidence. Five of the seven pastors reported an increase in leadership confidence as a direct result of recalibrating their churches. They indicated that while it takes courage to relaunch an established church, personal leadership confidence is often the first hurdle a leader must address.

Many factors tend to erode leadership confidence:

Age. Leaders worry that their age makes them irrelevant and no longer able to relate to their audience.

Team collaboration. One unintended consequence of team collaboration is that many times, leaders paralyze themselves with too much talk.

Failed attempts. A leader's confidence may have weakened due to previous failed attempts at revitalizing the church.

Emerging leaders. It is easy to feel your leadership confidence threatened by younger staff, a person you follow on social media, the coolest church plant down the street, or just your (unchanging) worldview. Read this carefully: While I believe in reverse mentoring, that seasoned leaders need to learn from younger leaders, YOU are the leader! They are not. So stop feeling threatened, fearful, or intimidated by emerging leaders, for in doing so, you forfeit your leadership. Listen to emerging leaders. Platform them in your church. But never forget: you are the leader and God has placed you where you are.

Ministry mistresses. Pastors, staff members, and even board members can hear the greatest preachers alive through social media. You can watch them, listen to podcasts, and obtain a flood of information. The allure of influence and prominence can become a seductive mistress, and pressure from your staff or supporters to be something other than your authentic self can feel overwhelming. Many leaders allow themselves to become discontented with their own skills and lose confidence, simply because they are constantly comparing themselves to the very best of someone else's ministry.

My heart for writing this book centers on this very issue. God wants to restore personal leadership confidence inside of *you!*

2. The feeling that your "best days" are behind you

This feeling, even if subtle, torments leaders, key influencers, and congregation members alike. It is easy to fall into this trap. If you often hear comments like, "I remember the days," or "I wish Sunday night would come back," recognize this as a red light flashing on your dashboard that's saying to you, "Your church needs to recalibrate."

This is not to say that it is wrong to honor tradition. Throughout this book, you'll hear that successful recalibration involves knowing your church's story. In order to understand the cultural DNA of an organization, it's necessary have a healthy appreciation for the efforts and investments of previous generations! What cannot be done, however, is to confuse *honoring* tradition with *worshiping* tradition.

Do you or your church feel as if your best days are behind you? If so, you're not alone; it's a normal and even expected part of a church's life cycle. Still, it is a flashing red light, signaling that the mission of your church has malfunctioned. It indicates that your church has been infected by mission drift, the deadly virus that will eventually cripple every part of your church body.

3. Ingrown culture

An ingrown culture is a clear flashing red light, signaling that a congregation needs to recalibrate. An ingrown culture will gradually kill your church body by slowly and methodically stifling your effectiveness and compassion. An ingrown church is its own standard of reference, making sure its members feel happy and comfortable and that the status quo is consistently maintained.

An ingrown culture is the most complex and difficult symptom to identify, but it puts your church into a comatose state. More importantly, it keeps your church from fulfilling the Great Commission. If you allow this virus to grow within your church, it will cause a plague that ends in congregational death.

Reggie McNeal provides a keen perspective on the true purpose of every church: "The church does not exist for itself. When it thinks it does, we've created a church-centric world. Our perception of reality is skewed. By external focus of ministry, I mean we radically reorient to understand that we exist primarily to do ministry beyond ourselves."[9] The church is the only organization alive that doesn't exist to take care of its own stakeholders. Rather, it exists to reach the people for whom Christ died.

The church has a far stronger tendency to become a swamp than a river. A swamp has restricted boundaries, fails to contribute to a broader body of water, and eventually begins to decay. A river always moves and changes, contributes to a greater body of water, and overflows with life.

Does your church smell like a swamp? Or does it have the fresh life of a river? Has your congregation become so ingrown that nothing new grows within it? Church leaders and influencers need to ask themselves a few questions to determine where they stand:

- What does your church budget tell you? Do you spend more money on placating Christians than on reaching the community?
- What does your church calendar tell you? Do your events entertain or empower Christians?
- What does your Sunday gathering tell you? Does it suggest a river or a swamp? Think about the language you use in your services, the attitudes of the people, and the overall "spiritual temperature" of the church. So many Sunday morning services are like visiting a family for dinner: anyone who comes in is an obvious stranger and is treated as such.
- Do you spend more time keeping people or reaching people? Be very truthful when you ask yourself this question!

Churches can become swamp-like almost overnight. The people in your congregation will tend naturally to focus on the four walls of your church. Left untreated, this virus will infect the way your people view *everything*.

4. Cultural and ministry misalignment

Cultural and ministry misalignment is one of the most common flashing red lights indicating a church needs to recalibrate. Misalignment refers to the incorrect arrangement or position of something in relation to something else.

Simply put, are your ministries arranged in such a way that they move the mission forward? Or do they stifle it? Over a period of time, your ministry model and programs *will* become misaligned. Your staff and your programs *will* start to work against each other, not with each other. People will start fighting over finances, volunteers, building usage, ministry promotion, or announcements . . . all so *their* ministry can have good numbers and success.

In chapter 7, I will speak in detail about the fatal attraction of most North American churches: cultural misalignment.

5. Plateaued or declining numbers

The recalibration process gets very sensitive here, but numerical growth is a part of diagnosing the health of a church. Take a hard, honest look at your numbers over the last five years. What do these numbers tell you about the condition of your church? Rainer believes that, "Churches with symptoms of sickness are likely to have declined or plateaued in worship attendance over the past five years."[10]

Many church leaders don't like to talk about this symptom. Who wants to admit his or her numbers have plateaued or are declining? Talking to a church about numbers is not unlike asking a person about his or her weight—a very sensitive topic on every level!

Nevertheless, the symptom of a decline in numbers signals that a church needs to recalibrate. Still, I can hear pastors now:

"It's not all about the numbers!"

"We may not be growing numerically, but we are growing spiritually deep."

"We have no interest in becoming a megachurch."

I both agree and disagree with such comments. When I get on a scale, the number I see means everything . . . and nothing. If I focus only on the number on the scale, I will never get healthy. I can weigh a "correct" number and still be dying of a deadly disease. I can be "deceptively healthy" while in grave danger of a heart attack. If I totally ignore the number, however, I am not living in reality.

Churches often rationalize their lack of growth with similar "spiritual" vernacular. By doing so, they forget that the numbers reveal a symptom of a problem, not the problem itself.

When leaders begin to disregard the numbers, it signifies that they are unwilling to face reality. Any attentive study of the book of Acts shows how the Spirit's work in the life of the church resulted in Kingdom expansion, both numerically and spiritually.[11]

The size of this book doesn't allow me to build a complete theology of numbers throughout Scripture. But it always amazes me how concerned God is about numbers. God told Moses to take a census of "the whole Israelite community by their clans and families, listing every man by name, one by one."[12] Luke gave careful attention to numbers throughout his history of the first years of the church. The Bible has a whole book called "Numbers," so let's not say numbers don't matter to God.

If your church suffers from this symptom, the proper treatment requires you to take an honest look at your numbers and ask, "What are they telling us?" Although numbers may reveal information from a symptomatic perspective, they do not always tell the whole story. Leaders need to consider four specific issues in diagnosing statistics:

Difficult decisions. Times exist when leaders must make difficult decisions that result in losing long-term church members, particularly during a relaunch or change initiative. This is the most difficult thing about recalibrating a church. It's painful and it's brutal, but it is a necessary reality.

Natural seasons. Churches go through natural stages of both growth and decline. Leaders need the wisdom to know what season they may be in, and then embrace these as part of the undercurrents of church life.

New church plants. When a church plants another church, this may have a negative impact on the home church's numbers.

Lack of community growth. My heart beats for churches in rural communities that may have limited opportunities for numerical growth.

My wife grew up in a small, rural church in Kingston, Idaho. She gave her life to Christ in that church, learned the Word of God there, and developed some of the greatest spiritual disciplines possible. This church was foundational to her spiritual development. She and I have talked about the many godly people who came out of this church: missionaries, pastors, and committed followers of Jesus all over the Northwest and the world. While this church may never experience numerical growth, it is having Kingdom impact in significant ways. My wife provides a living testimony that numbers don't tell the whole story.

> A church may be growing numerically, but still needs a cultural, holistic recalibration.

Leaders must consider genuine factors that impact growth in numbers, while simultaneously not permitting declines to camouflage a congregation's real deformities. While numbers don't tell the whole story, they may be a red light flashing at us, yelling, "Something is wrong!" The numbers often indicate that a church needs to recalibrate.

6. A lack of discipleship

Ironically, numbers themselves can camouflage and create a deceptively healthy church. Numbers can look fine while the church is off mission. A church may be growing numerically, but still needs a cultural, holistic recalibration. The greatest deception that leaders can fall prey to is measuring church health solely by bodies, budgets, and buildings, without regard to spiritual transformation.

In his book *Keeping Score: How to Know If Your Church Is Winning,* Dave Ferguson offers growing churches a strong warning: "A growing church attendance does not promise that people are growing spiritually. An attendance graph that is up and to the right does not guarantee that people are faithful in following Jesus and displaying the fruit of the Spirit in their lives."[13]

If the only (or primary) goal you have is to increase numbers, then you need to repent and recalibrate. Ferguson asserts that discipleship is the pursuit that matters most when diagnosing a church: "The challenge Jesus left with His followers is the same challenge He leaves with us, 'make disciples.'[14] This is what matters most—the making of disciples!" The church's mission does not aim to make consumers, fill seats, or develop sophisticated ministries.

The church does not exist to indulge Christians, but to make radical disciples who become Jesus' hands and feet to their community and world. At the end of the day, the only number that really counts is how many lives have been transformed through the ministry of your church. Jesus did not commission His church to make consumers, fill seats, or develop sophisticated ministries. Rather, He calls us to develop a passion to make radical disciples of Christ who passionately love God and one another and are empowered to go into their communities and world with the redemptive message of Jesus.

7. The diminishing noise of children

The diminishing noise of children in your nursery, children's church, or lobby is one of the most obvious and yet overlooked flashing red lights within a church. Whenever I perform an assessment of a Sunday service for a church, one of the first things I do is to visit the nursery. The nursery reveals everything about the future of the church.

If the nursery facilities are not well taken care of and the leaders and volunteers dread showing up, then know that you have discovered a flashing red light. Your church's nursery may be the number one indicator that you need to recalibrate.

> Your church's nursery may be the number one indicator that you need to recalibrate.

Think about the nursery in the context of your own home. When my wife and I had our first child, everything changed. Then we had our second child (about this time we started thinking a van might be a cool idea). When children come along, *everything* about your life changes: schedules, money, diapers, and sleepless nights. You baby-proof the house. You change the food you buy (and often eat). Everything!

My daughter got married and had twins. You think life changes with kids? Try twin grandbabies! You have to rethink, reset, reorganize, and recalibrate your entire home. No longer is this only about the adults; now it's about the kids.

At New Life, our nursery and children's ministry impact everything we do:

Service times. People often ask why we set service times at sixty-five to seventy minutes. It's not because we are trying to be cool and hip, but because we coordinate everything around our children's ministry. If the service goes seventy minutes, this means our volunteers are taking care of kids close to ninety-five to one hundred minutes. Kids typically get dropped off fifteen minutes before the service and picked up fifteen minutes afterward. With a seventy-minute service, that puts the average child in kids' ministry at about one hundred minutes (or one hour and forty minutes). This is a very long time for the nursery/children's workers! And you wonder why leaders in children's ministry are hard to recruit and retain, and sometimes can get negative?

Sunday school. We have a very limited adult Sunday school program because the kids need the rooms, and we need our adults to serve the kids. I would rather have adults serving our kids than simply sitting in a room, learning. This is a primary reason I so strongly believe in small groups outside of Sunday morning.

Budget. It amazes me how churches can spend thousands of dollars on a musical production, but make their kids' ministry do fundraisers! We canceled our Christmas musical after we decided to put our energy into a big Christmas event that honors family and kids, as opposed to doing yet another big church production.

Staffing. The most important person on your staff is your nursery director. Pastors often staff their churches with all types of positions before they staff their children's ministry. Such an approach is shortsighted and will stifle your growth opportunities with young families.

Stop Long Enough to Deal with the Red Light

We've all seen those lights come on, haven't we? Maybe it's the fuel light, and we hope we can squeeze out a few more miles. Maybe it's the washer fluid light, and we think, *Well, it's going to rain anyway!* The oil change light comes on, and we know we can knock out an extra few hundred miles. We ignore all the signs . . . and then we feel shocked when the whole thing breaks down, leaving us stranded on the side of the road in a downpour.

I hate it when any red light starts flashing in my car. It means I have to stop long enough to fix it. It means I have to interrupt my life and do something about it. I know it will probably cost me piles of money, and I don't really want to spend energy that I simply don't have.

It's easy to ignore the warning signs. It's easy to become deceptively healthy. People are happy, the budget is steady, and members congratulate you every so often on a well-crafted sermon. And so the church calendar ticks away from Easter to VBS to the Fall Festival to Christmas, all starting over again the next year.

It's time to get honest! It's time to stop blaming everyone and everything. I'm guessing that you're reading this book because you know, deep down, that something is wrong in your church. You may be deceptively healthy or even on life support, but you know something just isn't right.

Regardless where your church may be, remember that every church needs to recalibrate. It is not a matter of if, but when. So commit to recalibrate—because if you don't, your church will steadily and slowly drift off mission.

Coaching Assignments

1. Take some time to walk through the seven red lights. In your own words, define each red light. Perhaps add a few more that you may think about in your own cultural setting.

2. Personally ask yourself: "Where does my church show symptoms of needing to recalibrate? Does our church show signs of being deceptively healthy?" Be honest here!

3. Now involve key people in your church. Where does your church show symptoms of needing to recalibrate? Be honest! (Find some time and discuss this question with your spouse, board, key staff members, or handpicked people in your congregation.)

3

THE RECALIBRATION DANCE

About three years into my leadership at New Life, one of the "pillars" of the church asked to have coffee with me. I accepted, knowing he didn't feel happy with how things were going. As soon as we sat down, he started to express his laundry list of complaints:

The music was too loud.
I didn't care about older people.
I needed to revive adult Sunday school.
My new children's pastor had no clue.

Frankly, it all just made me angry. I got very defensive and every ounce of my sinful nature wanted to lash out. I simply couldn't stomach his complaints any longer. There we were, in the middle of a public restaurant, and I stood up, full of rage. "You don't know what the *hell* you are talking about!" Then I walked away. I felt hurt. I got defensive. I was angry.

As I climbed into my car, I recognized my behavior not only as sinful, but also disrespectful to our church's spiritual giants and faithful saints of the past. I knew I needed to resolve this wrong, so I called the vice-chairman of the elders (a primary influencer at New Life) and confessed my sin to him. Graciously, he called the offended pillar of New Life and set up a meeting between the three of us.

When we gathered, I confessed my sin to this man and asked for his forgiveness. By God's grace, he forgave me. Although it took years to rebuild trust in this relationship, God did eventually restore our love for each other. I thank God that he is still an important part of our New Life family.

As this story might suggest, my first three years of leading New Life were among the toughest of my life. Conflicts like this occurred repeatedly. I remember when the top giver in the church looked me straight in the eyes and told me he was leaving over some "meaningless" issue. How painful that felt! How I wanted to point my finger and call these people modern-day Pharisees! I could have blamed everything and everyone for the turmoil I faced as pastor.

As I look back at this stormy season of life, however, I now see it as a turning point for my leadership. The Achilles heel of the church was *me*. An Achilles heel is a deadly weakness despite overall strength, potentially serious enough to lead to downfall.

Eventually I came to understand that I needed to learn the art of leading an established church. I needed to see leading change as a dance with the people I love, not as a war with the people who oppose me. And that meant that I had to approach the process in phases, not in one giant step.

Change Your Metaphor

As I analyzed what happened at New Life and spent time examining the ups and downs of recalibrating our church, I identified three distinct phases I that I now refer to as the "Recalibration Dance." These three phases remain true whether you are leading a cultural recalibration or targeting a specific ministry, system, or leadership practice.

Recalibrating your church is both an organized, intentional discipline and an organic, intuitive dance. It involves planned and deliberate, step-by-step phases as well as the living, instinctual sense to know when the music is playing and you need to lead the congregation in a new dance.

Recalibrating your church is an:

Organized and intentional discipline: There is a science and discipline behind recalibrating an organization, utilizing a planned and easy-to-understand sequential order.

Organic and intuitive dance: Recalibration is an invitation to dance with the congregation you love, not marching to a war with foes you must conquer. You lead with grace.

Far too often, leaders approach effecting change as if they were in a war zone instead of on a dance floor. I go to war with my enemies; I dance with my loved ones. Recalibrating your church is a beautiful dance with the board, staff, influencers, and entire church, not a skirmish with a stubborn enemy. Dancing isn't always easy, however! Remember a few hard facts about dancing: You will step on people's toes. Someone has to lead in the dance without being a bully. Dancing requires both organized steps and organic strides.

> **Recalibrating your church is both an organized, intentional discipline and an organic, intuitive dance.**

While principles and practices make the recalibration process possible, the leader also has to listen to the heart of God and discern the timing of the congregation. Leaders must listen to the music or sound of the congregation, and most importantly, to the music of God's direction. They must be willing to back up and then step forward at the right moment and time. The dance goes back and forth—sometimes in a sequential order, but more often than not requiring the dancers to step back and forth between assessment, alignment, and action. Leaders must honor their partner, trying to be graceful yet clear on the order of the dance.

The following diagram illustrates the Recalibration Dance:

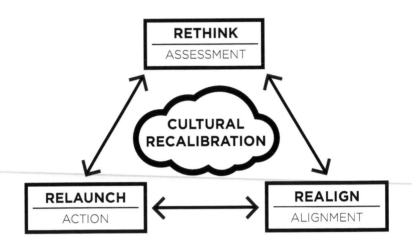

The boxes represent the organized and intentional discipline of recalibration, while the arrows symbolize the organic and intuitive dance of cultural recalibration. You are always moving back and forth between phases. One moment you are rethinking your church; the next moment you may be realigning. One moment you are ready to relaunch and take action, and then instead you find yourself rethinking your original plan.

This chapter outlines the three phases of the Recalibration Dance, which are: Rethink, Realign, and Relaunch. Let's look more closely at each of these phases in greater detail.

The Rethink Phase: Challenge the Status Quo

The first phase of recalibrating your church or organization is the Rethink Phase. During this phase, leaders honestly assess their leadership and congregation. Every recalibration starts with challenging the status quo and asking probing and piercing questions—no sacred cows, personal agendas, or attacking people—*everything* is on the table.

This is the time the leader stops playing games and making excuses and instead insists, "It is time to rethink everything." Walking in a daze from Sunday to Sunday is no longer an option. It is time to step up or step away.

In their book Replant: *How a Dying Church Can Grow Again*, Darrin Patrick and Mark DeVine tell of how God turned around a historic church located in a beautiful building in downtown Kansas City. They communicate the attitude and resolve needed in order to recalibrate a church: "At some point, leaders in a declining or plateauing church have to look at themselves in the mirror and say, 'Enough is enough.' Leaders need clarity about what the Scripture says the church ought to be, and courage to stand against those who refuse to let the Scripture inform their view of the church."[15]

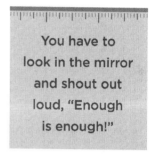

You have to look in the mirror and shout out loud, "Enough is enough!"

You have to be bold enough to say, "Enough is enough!" You have to look in the mirror and shout out loud, "Enough is enough! I am sick of my church being ingrown, entrenched, and ineffective. I am done with seeing no one being transformed by the power of the gospel. With God's help, I am going to lead this church into the future."

Are you sick and tired of the status quo in your church? Really? I have discovered it often takes years or even decades before some leaders can find enough courage and confidence to rethink the status quo. Oftentimes, some deep emotional and spiritual preparation must occur before he or she is ready even to begin. No one can force the leader to be ready. I believe God is the only one who can prepare the leader for changes of this magnitude.

When we accept the status quo, we accept a death sentence on our churches or organizations. Let those words sink in. If you accept the status quo, you are in effect inviting its termination. Howard Schultz, the chairman and CEO of Starbucks, firmly believes that leaders must confront the status quo, or they will die: "We cannot be content with the status quo. Any business today that embraces the status quo as an operating principle is going to be on a death march."[16]

You have to make some tough, emotional decisions that can feel absolutely brutal. You have to allow them to burn in your heart. Recalibrating your church needs to become very personal for you.

You need to say about your church and your leadership:

- Enough with complacency and safe living!
- Enough with the status quo and business as usual!
- Enough with an inward, selfish, consumerist mindset about Christianity!
- Enough of allowing my community to go to hell while Christians fight over insignificant doctrinal issues!

The Realign Phase: Infuse New Cultural DNA into Your Church

The second phase of recalibration is by far the most difficult. It's where most leaders take shortcuts and tend to step on the toes of everyone with whom they're dancing. During the Realign Phase, the leader infuses new cultural DNA into the church.

Recalibration is not merely a cosmetic change, but a cultural shift that resets the organization from the inside out. Recalibrating your church will fail miserably if you don't infuse new cultural DNA into your congregation.

Do you know anyone who has had an organ transplant? These individuals have to take a series of drugs to prevent their bodies from rejecting the new organ, even though that organ is there to save their lives. Why the drugs? Because the DNA of the new organ doesn't match the person's own DNA.

In a similar way, and in a very real sense, you have to give your church a series of "drugs" to prevent your congregational body from rejecting the new "organ." You have to avoid the common error that imagines that if you do a few "cool" things, then the church will automatically grow.

You have to reject several typical misunderstandings:

- If you write out a mission statement and a few core values, everything changes.
- Adding a "contemporary service" results in automatic growth.
- Turning up (or down) the music will result in people lining up to get into your church.
- Wear skinny jeans, and Jesus will show up.
- People will flock to your services if you offer coffee in the lobby.

At best, all of these are band-aid solutions that *may* catch the attention of your people, but more likely, they'll just cause a lot of frustration. Don't misunderstand me! New Life does most of these things (although wearing skinny jeans is *not* at the top of the list). But these things, by themselves, will only cause problems if you fail to realign and transform the culture. If you don't realign your culture, all your efforts at recalibrating your church will amount to nothing more than a passing fad and another failed scheme the desperate pastor dreamed up.

In his book *Leading Change*, John Kotter offers an eight-stage process of leading change. He believes that neglecting to anchor change in the corporate culture inevitably results in failure. Kotter clearly identifies the depth of the cultural change: "In the final analysis, change sticks only when it becomes 'the way we do things around here,' when it seeps into the very bloodstream of the work unit or corporate body."[17]

Think of your church as something like a computer. Every computer has two crucial components:

- *Hardware:* The physical computer. This includes the motherboard, the hard drive and the processor.
- *Operating systems:* The system software (OS) that manages computer hardware and software resources. This software tells the hardware how to function and what to do. The OS provides common services for computer programs. Most software and applications programs usually require an operating system.

Your organization runs a lot like a computer. It has an operating system that runs in the background of everything. In leadership terms, I refer to this as the cultural operating system (COS). It includes your assumptions, values, and systems—the bedrock processes that allow you to do church.

This COS sends signals and determines everything:

- How programs are designed
- How ministry is organized
- How preachers preach
- How decisions are made

Your COS includes all the underlying assumptions about your church. Although it's almost entirely invisible, it determines what you value, talk about, celebrate, assume, and how you make decisions. In everything we do, we have underlying assumptions.

This helps to explain why so many churches that have tried to turn around their churches or revitalize their congregations have failed. The reason is fairly simple to grasp. They neglected to change, or even to take into account, their old COS.

You can't add the latest software (new service, music style, etc.) to an out-of-date COS and then expect them to work! Just because you stopped wearing a tie on Sunday morning doesn't mean that you're now a "relevant" church. Just because you changed the name of your church or updated your website doesn't mean these changes will work, *unless* you also change the COS.

Many churches run Windows 98 in a Windows 10 world. They are trying to change their music style without changing their COS. You have to upgrade your COS to remain effective in ministry.

When you transform the culture, you transform the church.

If you ignore culture, you get crucified.

The only way to transform the culture is to upgrade to a new COS and intentionally, carefully create a new culture of continuous recalibration. Once you create this culture of recalibration and infuse new cultural practices, the church will begin to undergo a deep, cultural change.

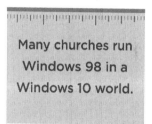
Many churches run Windows 98 in a Windows 10 world.

According to Kim Cameron and Robert Quinn in their book *Diagnosing and Changing Organizational Culture*, "The concept of culture refers to the taken-for-granted values, underlying assumptions, expectations, and definitions that characterize organizations and their members."[18] I define COS as the underlying assumptions and values in an organization as expressed in shared enthusiasm, common language, and aligned practices. In any organization with a healthy and well-defined culture, you immediately observe the intangible connection between what the organization champions, speaks, and celebrates.

It is easy to cop out and say that since people resist change, there is no hope for your church or organization. While it is true that many people resist change, the core issue is a cultural problem, not resistance to change itself.

In chapter 6, I will outline what I call the Four Quadrants of Change. This will help you to distinguish the difference between what I call load-bearing and non-load-bearing cultural changes. But the bottom line is that some changes are easier to make than others. People tend to resist *cultural* change, not *all* change.

Gordon MacDonald wrote a very helpful book for leaders who want to recalibrate their church, titled *Who Stole My Church?*[19] This classic helps leaders understand the power of culture and how people will feel when leaders make changes. In his fictional story, McDonald describes how a new pastor brought changes to his congregation. At first, the congregation wanted and welcomed these changes. A problem arose, however, when the congregation realized that instead of expected program changes, it was getting a cultural transformation. MacDonald explains how the people expected "merely a fresh voice in the pulpit and a program or two imported from more successful churches."[20] The pastor underestimated the cultural shift:

> Whenever a culture shift occurs at a church, people will feel it deeply and personally.

> "What he and his fellow church members had not anticipated was a total shift in the church's culture, a reinvention (a favorite word of mine) of ways to love God and serve people. What they did not see coming was a reshuffling of the church's priorities, so that lost and broken people rather than found and supposedly fixed people became the primary target audience."[21]

During a cultural recalibration, many people will feel as though someone has stolen their church. They will feel cheated, lied to, violated, and ripped off. Understanding culture gives leaders the necessary patience to deal with congregants who have a difficult time with cultural transitions.

Leaders who understand the subtleties of culture won't feel disoriented by change, frustrated by opposition, or stymied by misunderstanding. Whenever a culture shift occurs at a church, people will feel it deeply and personally.

Understanding issues through a cultural lens is essential when responding to frustration, senseless comments, knee-jerk pushbacks, and loud verbal processing. Understanding culture helps to embed grace into the hearts of leaders and helps them patiently lead people who naturally resist change. This allows leaders to extend grace toward the very people we sometimes label as "Pharisees," "older brothers," and "critics."

Leaders often like to throw anyone who opposes suggested changes into some Pharisaical bucket. I don't trust arrogant leaders who make comments like, "If you don't like our changes, then you can leave my church—and don't let the door hit you on your way out," or "Those Christians are acting just like Pharisees." I am no therapist or analyst, but in my uneducated opinion, these leaders like to talk big and hide behind these childish statements.

This kind of behavior is not fair. In fact, it is childish and flat-out wrong. No doubt there *are* Pharisees in your church (that's another book). But just because someone complains, expresses concerns, or shows any kind of pushback doesn't place them in the same category as the Pharisees who opposed Jesus.

Never confuse disagreement with disloyalty! The father in the parable of the prodigal son graciously led the older brother. He didn't say, "Get out of my house, you rebel. You have an unteachable spirit!" Rather, he calmly and lovingly reminded the brother of why the celebration had occurred in the first place, namely, "that which was lost is now found."

Leaders have to learn to see critics through a cultural lens and not as personal attackers. They need to remember that congregants have learned their church culture over many years, even decades, and that it will take time to absorb a new one.

The Relaunch Phase: Stop Tinkering with Change and Do It

This is where the rubber meets the road. This is where you hit the tarmac. This is where you begin actually moving your feet and dancing with your congregation. This is the moment where a leader has to step up and stop tinkering with change and just do it.

You put everything on the line.

You pull the trigger.

You turn the vision into reality.

It's time for the tipping point of your congregation, when everything changes in the blink of eye—the moment of critical mass, the threshold, the boiling point. It's time for action and execution—no more talk!

I have discovered in speaking with many staff members, associates, and even spouses of leaders that many feel this deep frustration. "I am sick of hearing and talking about these ideas," they say. "Make a decision! Do something!" In effect, they are saying, "Execute the plan!"

Far too many leaders "talk, talk, talk," without taking action. People want action. Inaction also strengthens the criticisms of doubters and naysayers, who will scoff and say, "I told you so."

Change cannot come through inaction. Execution requires that you date it, define it, and do it. In chapter 12 I will discuss in detail how to hit the tarmac and execute your Relaunch Initiative.

One of the books that greatly influenced my doctoral dissertation and my overall conclusions is titled Influencer: *The New Science of Leading Change*. The authors, best known for their work on the book *Crucial Conversations*, warn against the dangers of "tinkering" with change: "Whatever the rationale for tinkering, the cost of putting forth a tepid effort can be extraordinary. In addition to the fact that addressing profound problems with trivial solutions doesn't create the changes you desire, you do create a reputation for not being able to create change."[22] Tinkering with change will never cultivate momentum and move a church forward.

The relaunch metaphor provides a word picture for execution and implies full energy and focus. Relaunching speaks of an increased amount of energy and intentionality, focusing the church long enough to trigger a mission, vision, and cultural shift. As a verb, "relaunch" means to launch again, start, or get going.[23] Think in terms of an airplane. The plane expends the greatest amount of fuel and energy when it takes off (or "launches"). On short flights, as much as 25 percent of the total fuel consumed gets used during this time.[24]

During the Relaunch Phase, the leader focuses all available energy and resources to catapult the church or organization to new heights. The leader declares this to be a new chapter for the church and rallies the church to action. This is where most people err in recalibrating. There has to be a tipping point, a definite moment where people can say, "From this day forward, our church is different."

Date It. Define It. Do It.

Leaders need a model, a vehicle, for leading change. I call this model the Relaunch Initiative.

It is one thing to have a clear and compelling vision; it is an entirely different thing to have a clear and working vehicle to turn this vision into a reality.

I live in Seattle, Washington. Any farther north and you're in Canada; any farther west and you're in Japan. Every time I take a trip, it seems like it takes forever to get there. Anyone traveling from Seattle wishes they could use a *Star Wars* hyperdrive.

But my wife and I do enjoy traveling, so vacations together are an important part of our relationship.

Anytime I go on vacation, I have two basic questions to answer:

- Where will we go? (vision)
- How will we get there? (vehicle)

If I wanted to get to New York, the first thing I would do is decide on my vehicle. I could ride a horse and take months. I could drive and take forty-three hours. I could fly and take a few hours.

The vehicle you choose is critical. Many churches are still using dated vehicles of change that no longer work. They're using a horse and buggy in a day of jet travel.

The vehicle for recalibrating your church is the Relaunch Initiative. A Relaunch Initiative is a time-bound, well-defined, mission-critical initiative that serves as a catalyst to recalibrate your church. The business world refers to this as a strategic initiative, a change initiative, or an innovative strategy.

Leadership guru Peter Drucker, who contributed enormously to the philosophical and practical foundations of the modern business corporation, argues in his book *Managing the Non-Profit Organization* that organizations need an "innovative strategy, a way to bring the new to the marketplace."[25] Relaunch initiatives provide a practical approach for the leader to bring something new to the congregation.

> Somewhere along the line, leaders have to stop *talking* about recalibrating their churches, put a precise date on the calendar, and *do it.*

Drucker further reminds us that all the good intentions in the world won't create a bit of change. "There is an old saying that good intentions don't move mountains; bulldozers do," he writes. "In nonprofit management, the mission and the plan, if that's all there is, are the good intentions. Strategies are the bulldozers. They convert what you want to do into accomplishment."[26]

During a Relaunch Initiative, leaders hit the tarmac and do three practical things: they date it, define it, and do it.

In chapter 12, I will suggest:

- Three practical things to consider when deciding your relaunch date

- Seven elements to consider when defining your Relaunch Initiative
- Five practical things to do during a Relaunch Initiative

For now, let's focus on the concept of "Date it. Define it. Do it" and how this influences your Relaunch Initiative.

1. Date it

I thought about calling this entire book, *Date It!* I considered that title because until you put a date on it, you are only talking.

Somewhere along the line, leaders have to stop talking about recalibrating their churches, put a precise date on the calendar, and *do it*. Talk is cheap. You cultivate catalytic tipping points with a date, not with a bunch of discussion. Until a leader sets a date, saying, "This is the moment when God is going to do something new in our church; this is a tipping point," he or she is only talking philosophy. That church will never recalibrate. When a leader says, "Here is the date when we will relaunch our church," then recalibration can begin to take place.

The authors of *Influencer* discuss how "fuzzy and unclear goals" will never move an organization forward. They also discuss the immediate power of time-bound targets: "The effect of providing this clear, compelling, and time-bound target was immediate. It started a whole chain of events that virtually redefined the organization."[27]

When you set a precise date and then publicly announce it to your staff, board, and key influencers, a chain reaction will begin. A few years ago, when I said to my team, "On February 12, 2012, everything will change at New Life," the announcement started a chain reaction that prompted excitement and growth. When you announce a date, some things almost immediately begin to happen.

Setting a date does a number of things in the hearts and souls of leaders and their churches:

A date forces a leader to stop talking about change and do it. Something changes in the hearts of leaders when they say, "In 280 days, I am putting a stake in the ground and leading us in an initiative of innovation and change." The date makes a difference. It creates energy.

A date starts a chain of events that redefines everything. The date forces people into action. It makes people say to themselves, "This is real." It begins a chain reaction that results in action and people getting things done. It is the first domino. Once you push this one, it affects everything in your congregation.

A date takes the conversation from philosophical to practical. Far too many leaders get caught in the "philosophical trap." The moment a leader sets a date, however, everything changes. No longer is this merely a philosophical conversation. This now becomes real. The church will recalibrate.

2. Define it

Many leaders tend to speak in vague terms. They are masters of speaking in generalities. But generalizations will never move a church forward. People need clarity on every level.

No doubt it is easier to say, "God wants to bless our church," than it is to set a precise date and say, "On this day, we are going to recalibrate our church. Here are the specific initiatives we are trusting God to do." Your church will move forward only when you are clear, not vague.

When I am vague, people listen (but that's all). When I am clear, people get things done. It is just that simple.

The authors of *Influencer* describe the result of a clear, compelling, and challenging initiative. Read this carefully and slowly:

"Clear goals aimed at a compelling target can have an enormous impact on behavior because they engage more than simply the brain. They also engage the heart. Research reveals that a clear, compelling, and challenging goal causes the blood to pump more rapidly, the brain to fire, and the muscles to engage. However, when goals are vague, no such effects take place."[28]

Relaunch initiatives will cause the blood to pump more rapidly in your church, the brain to fire, and all the muscles to engage. Prepare yourself for your people to actually engage, get fired up, and prepare to cross the Red Sea with you!

3. Do it

This is where you stop talking about the change initiative and you do it. In many ways, this is where the rubber meets the road. You have to cross the finish line. You have to do it, or it's just a bunch of talk that will frustrate everyone. Again, in chapter 12, I will suggest five practical actions for leaders to take during a Relaunch Initiative.

Take a Deep Breath and Have Fun

When my daughter got married a few years ago, it was the first time I ever thought about taking dancing seriously. I took dance classes just to prepare for the "catalytic" moment.

I felt awkward. Everything about it seemed out of place. But she was beautiful! So the moment that the DJ announced the father-daughter dance, I had to take a deep breath and say, "This is about her." I had to take a deep breath and just have fun. I was determined to enjoy the moment.

I couldn't let the probability that I might step on her toes stop me—nor the fact that I have no rhythm. While I won no awards for best father-daughter dance of the year, this was a meaningful and significant event for my daughter.

I know you might be saying, "Listen, you haven't met my board or congregation." I get it. They don't wear a beautiful white dress or look into your eyes with the love of a daughter. But *you* should! You should look into their eyes with a deep love, take a deep breath, and have fun.

Enjoy your church!

Dance with your church!

Take a deep breath and have fun!

Coaching Assignments

1. Review the three phases of the Recalibration Dance. Why is a cultural recalibration both an organized, intentional discipline and an organic, intuitive dance? Assess your own leadership personality. Do you tend to be overly organized in leading your church or overly organic in your leadership style?

2. Of the three phases of cultural recalibration, which phase requires the most courage for you and your church? Which phase is the most difficult for you to lead and process? Why?

3. If you were to relaunch your church, what is the precise date you would do this? At this point, look at your church cadence. I have found February or late September are the best times to relaunch a congregation.

Part Two

THE RETHINK PHASE: CHALLENGE THE STATUS QUO

The first part of the Recalibration Dance is what I call the "Rethink Phase." In the Rethink Phase, leaders confront the status quo and do an honest, gut-level assessment of where they are as a church and as leaders.

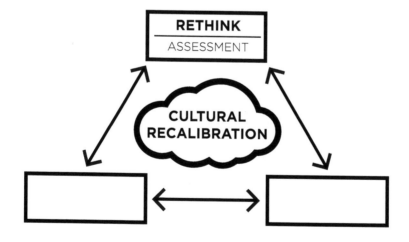

In this section, I will discus three of the nine leadership practices to recalibrate your church. I call these the Rethink Practices.

- *Practice #1* | Confront the Status Quo:
  Ask Probing and Piercing Questions
- *Practice #2* | Clarify Non-Negotiables:
  Preserve the Core, Yet Stimulate Progress
- *Practice #3* | Think Mission Critical:
  Change Only What You Have to Change

The goal of the Rethink Phase is to diagnose the condition of your church and develop a time-bound, well-defined, and mission-critical Relaunch Initiative.

While you start with an honest assessment of your church, the goal is not merely philosophical in nature, but practical in nature. The goal is to turn the vision into reality!

Rethinking your church will require you to stretch your leadership muscles in ways you never thought possible. When you start stretching these leadership muscles, initially you will feel real pain, just like when you begin to exercise muscles you have never used or haven't used in a long time. The Rethink Phase of recalibrating your church takes time. It takes sweat. And it brings pain.

But it is worth the pain.

It is worth the process.

It is worth the risk of hearing things you don't want to hear or face.

4

PRACTICE #1
CONFRONT THE STATUS QUO:
Ask Probing and Piercing Questions

The first step in an honest assessment of your congregation is to ask probing and piercing questions. The Rethink Phase begins with the leader taking a deep breath and asking the hard questions, knowing that it will cause some tension in the room and make everyone feel uncomfortable.

Everyone feels awkward during the Rethink Phase. Your board will feel tension. Your staff will push back. Your influencers will ask hard questions. Even you will suffer some heartburn.

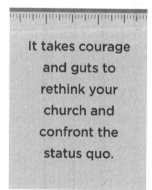

It takes courage and guts to rethink your church and confront the status quo.

It's painful, yes, but recognize that no doctor or therapist ever diagnosed a client without asking uncomfortable questions. Imagine a doctor who had a patient with a hacking cough, but who felt too embarrassed to ask if the individual was a smoker. Therapists would never help anyone if they thought a question like, "How's your sex life?" was too confrontational. Discomfort goes with the territory.

There just is no way around it. It takes courage and guts to rethink your church and confront the status quo.

Let's All Be Positive

Leaders often ask what I call "safe and secure" questions, as opposed to "probing and piercing" questions. There is a huge difference. A safe and secure question defends the status quo, secures tradition, and seeks comfortable answers:

"How do we compare to the church down the street?"

"How do we keep our members happy and content?"

"How can we change with the least amount of negative impact?"

For most of us, the truth feels uncomfortable and perhaps even negative. It is, however, the place where cultural change begins to happen.

Probing and piercing questions often feel negative. Deceptively healthy churches tend to hide behind the camouflage of "Let's all be positive." But there is a big difference between negative and pessimistic questions versus probing and piercing questions. Negative questions address issues passively, defend perceived territories, and look to assign blame.

Samuel Chand has contributed greatly to the Church's perspective of culture in his book, *Cracking Your Church's Culture Code*. He depicts how change agents ask piercing questions: "Change agents need to be positive, but they need to be multidimensional: they must also possess the ability to ask penetrating questions to help the group discern God's will, to find the best alignment of roles and goals, and to develop the best plan for any challenge."[29]

The difference is found in the "why" behind the question. If you ask probing and piercing questions in order to complain, get your way, or win support for some hidden, selfish agenda, then you are administering poison to your congregation. The main reason to ask probing and piercing questions is to move the mission forward, not to try to get your own way or to defend your position.

Rethinking your church requires asking the difficult questions that uncover brutal realities. Such questions reject church comparisons and create necessary tension.

Asking probing and piercing questions will:

- Open up conversations and get critical issues on the table.
- Cut through the surface and move the mission forward.
- Deal with current realities, not fantasies.
- Expose pitfalls.
- Slice through the fog.
- Reset your values.
- Intentionally create points of tension.

Don't Commit Malpractice

It's easy to read a book or go to some conference and return home with a new plan for your congregation without first doing a proper assessment of where the church is and where it should go. But it is a fatal mistake to lay out a Relaunch Initiative without first putting the proper work into diagnosing your current context and culture.

Recalibrating your church or organization requires careful thought and prayerful analysis. It is inexcusable to prescribe an action plan without a proper diagnosis.

Imagine a doctor attempting to prescribe medication to a patient simply because the physician saw it work somewhere else. He would get sued for malpractice! Instead, responsible doctors ask a series of questions about family history, allergies, lifestyle, and dozens of other topics. Doctors know that they must tailor each diagnosis to fit each patient. I have a friend who is allergic to the most common antibiotic on the planet, penicillin. If a doctor prescribed what worked for everyone else to help him, my friend would die in minutes. Great doctors take the time to diagnose properly.

Great leaders do the same thing. When it comes time to prescribe a new course of action for an organization, they recognize that they must custom fit the solution. This is another area where leading an established church is radically different from planting a church. You must consider the culture, content, and environment you are working with.

Every church differs from every other church. Every leader has different gifts and passions, every culture has different nuances and traditions, and every community has different needs and challenges. It is fatal to prescribe before you diagnose.

I remember exactly where I was sitting when I read the following quote from *Influencer: The New Science of Leading Change:* "Diagnose before you prescribe. Anything else is malpractice. Most leaders fail to take this essential step and simply throw together an influence strategy they believe should work under any circumstances."[30] I literally stood up and started to clap. Every church leader needs to internalize this insight!

Novice leaders throw together a strategy without first praying, thinking, and grounding the proposed changes in Scripture. They seek quick fixes and flashy solutions, all the while ignoring the fundamental flaws in their cultural DNA. Don't make the mistake of prescribing some currently popular solution for your unique problems.

Three Starting Points

I am about to suggest five probing and piercing questions you can ask to help diagnose your church. Before you jump into these questions, however, consider three starting points that will help you to confront the status quo of your church.

1. Embrace your humanity

Very few people are willing to admit it, but most leaders get defensive and take things personally when the organizations they lead get subjected to close examination.

It's normal to feel insecure. It's normal to get defensive. I call this "humanity."

It is *very* easy to get defensive and start blaming people and circumstances during the Rethink Phase of recalibration! Have you ever found yourself saying or at least feeling these emotions?

- Why are "they" planting a new church by my church?
- My staff doesn't get it (I just can't find good staff).
- The board is controlling.
- The pillars of the church are unwilling to change.
- The money we need isn't there.
- The new church plant down the street is taking all the good people.
- The devil is attacking my church.

Those who deny their basic human reactions are not being honest. At times, I hear leaders say, "I never get defensive," or "I have no problem with candid input." While I appreciate the attempt to suppress their humanity, it's a lost cause. Leaders *must* address and embrace their humanity. To deny your natural, human responses to change (especially when those suggested changes appear to fault you in some way) is not a realistic way to move forward.

> **Don't make the mistake of prescribing some currently popular solution for your unique problems.**

I remember how I reacted when people started talking to me about my style of dress for Sunday services. Talk about defensive! I put up all the normal defensive mechanisms: "This is shallow thinking," "I am deeper than this," and the list goes on. Do you know the truth? I simply don't like talking about my faults, shortcomings, or any obstacle in the church for which I might bear some responsibility. I get defensive. I feel insecure.

While all this is true, I just refuse (most of the time) to let my humanity stop me from confronting the status quo. The future of the church is more important to me than my own insecurities and feelings.

I am no therapist, but from my perspective, the healthiest way to combat these emotions is to identify them and call them into the light. Admit you feel this way (if you do), and begin to deconstruct the emotion and reveal the truth. By identifying these thoughts and confronting them, you can begin to move beyond the normal pitfalls and barriers to fulfilling God's vision for your church.

So take a deep breath and relax. Ask God for the humility and character you need to navigate your own insecurity and natural tendencies to get defensive. The future of your church is at stake! Don't let your humanity get in the way of dealing with the status quo of your church.

2. Get outside perspective

I remember it as if it happened only yesterday. I brought in a leader to provide me with some observations about our weekend gatherings. The truth is, I really thought he would shower me and my team with praise. He came for an entire weekend and walked around and asked a lot of questions. He walked our parking lot, lobby, children's ministry, auditorium, and every part of our church. I felt so excited! I couldn't wait to hear his reflections.

We sat down at a local restaurant that Sunday night and he handed me a ten-page document. That in itself surprised me—how could he compliment us for ten full pages? The first part of our meeting felt very positive. He listed some of the key things that New Life was doing right. Then he looked at me and said, "Would you like to know some areas to improve?" With great excitement, I replied, "Yes!"

For the next two hours, he pointed out detail after detail of where New Life needed to improve, areas that were not nearly so strong as I had perceived them to be. He noted faulty systems that we had grown so accustomed to using that I no longer even noticed them.

At first, I wanted to get defensive. I wanted to explain why this system looked like that and why that program took this shape—you know, give him "context." But I refrained. I just listened. And by the end of that day, we decided New Life needed to recalibrate once again.

Recalibration often requires outside perspective. We get so used to our own "smell" that we don't even smell it anymore. Every leader needs fresh eyes and outside perspective.

Consider the process of selling your house. If I ever sold my house, who would provide me insights to get it ready to sell? The answer is obvious. I need an outsider to take a critical look and help me see what I don't see. The truth is, I have accepted the flaws of my house. I live in my house every day. All the smells—the candles, the detergent and dryer sheets, my wife's perfume, and the dog's scent—are second nature to me. I have lived there for so long that I don't see the things that scream, "DON'T BUY ME!" The smell of my house no longer fazes me.

Church leaders often have a subtle theology that proclaims, "All I need is God," or "If I pray more, the church will have full Kingdom impact." We think, *The Bible already tells me everything I need to know.* And at first glance, such statements sound very spiritual, but they reveal a serious theological flaw that will lead you down a road of isolation and discouragement.

As a part of my academic work, I developed a theological foundation for recalibration that includes the biblical notion that God chooses to speak through other people to provide us with fresh eyes and to identify blind spots in our lives.

Throughout Scripture, we see leaders who relied on others for a fresh perspective. When overwhelmed by the duties of management and leadership, Moses sought counsel from Jethro. When David lost sight of his failure and morality, the prophet Nathan called him back. When the church was being split over ethnic identity and doctrinal distractions, God brought Peter and James together to establish a new understanding.

> **Leaders need trusted people who provide them with feedback on the overall direction and vision of the church.**

While leaders need to hear from God directly, they fool themselves if they do not understand that God provides wisdom, direction, correction, and encouragement through others. Leaders need trusted people who provide them with feedback on the overall direction and vision of the church. These people offer fresh eyes for identifying ministry philosophies that are hurting Kingdom impact, poor organizational structures, faulty decision processes, and outdated church systems.

One of the fundamental challenges leaders face is how to find these trusted other voices. Let me suggest a few options to consider:

Find a leadership coach. I understand this can be very difficult. This coach may be someone widely recognized as a coach or a trusted leader. This may be a professional consultant or someone with whom you have a trusted relationship. Many people in the business world would love to provide a congregation with some new insight and perspective.

Visit another church. It always shocks me to discover how many church leaders never visit other churches for the sake of getting outside perspective. Of course, I get the challenges of doing this. Leaving your church on Sundays is difficult. Who will preach? Do worship? While all these are issues, taking time to see other approaches to church programming provides great benefits.

Attend a conference. Hearing the wisdom of well-known church leaders is only one of the benefits of attending a conference. You also can create new relationships of encouragement and exhortation with fellow attendees. And it helps to take some time away from the cycle of ongoing church services to gain some helpful reflection and perspective.

Listen to outsiders. This may seem counter-intuitive, but some of the best perspective you can get on your church comes from people who don't regularly go there. They have no territories to defend, investments to honor, or traditions to uphold. Take a non-Christian friend to coffee and ask him what kind of church he would go to. Use follow-up cards from first or second-time visitors. Go to a local coffee shop one day a week and listen to the people in your area. In our attempts to develop great Christian relationships, how often do we hear from the very people we are trying to reach?

Read. Charlie "Tremendous" Jones said it best: "The only difference between where you are today, and where you'll be a year from today, are the books you read and the people you meet."[31] Reading books, magazines, blogs, and online articles, watching TED Talks—all these are ways to gain access to great leaders, innovative thinkers, and organizational coaches without having to spend thousands. Pay attention to what you read! Read from a variety of disciplines and fields of study, not just your own. Take notes and share your insights.

Get outside of your tribe. My tribe is the Assemblies of God. While I have benefited greatly from being a part of this tribe, New Life never would have seen its growth and Kingdom impact had I limited myself to my tribe. Leaders must have enough humility to understand that they don't have all the answers and perspectives that they require.

The bottom line is that every leader needs outside perspective. I know it may cost money to find that outside perspective. It can be expensive to find a coach or consultant, fly to another church, or even attend a conference. But let me be very clear: the money you lose by not finding an outside perspective will far outstrip the money you save by failing to invest in this discipline. The truth is, you have been at your church for so long that you can no longer clearly see its shortcomings. You need outside perspective.

3. Involve the right people

To adequately confront the status quo, you need to involve the right people in the Rethink/Assessment Phase. It is foolish to confront the status quo by yourself and then announce all the changes you've decided to make to your staff, board, influencers, and the church. You're asking for a train wreck! You need to involve the right people in this discussion.

The people around you will determine the effectiveness of every change initiative in your church. You cannot do this alone! People often resist and ultimately refuse change simply because nobody involved them in the change initiative, or even bothered to communicate to them the "why" behind the change.

We wrestle and agonize with changes God is birthing in our hearts, sometimes for months or even years. We read, discuss, process, and allow ourselves time to push back and ask questions. Then in one sitting, we announce the huge cultural change coming to our churches. We expect the people to say, "Yes, let's all just accept this now and change!"

Leaders usually allow themselves time to process, but if anyone else dares to verbally process the change, asks too many questions, or struggles with doubts, these leaders too often label them as naysayers or quenchers of the Spirit. Why are we shocked that people need the same time to process and push back that we gave ourselves? Why does it surprise us that people need time to ask questions, process, and wrestle with the proposed changes?

Remember, these people are the stakeholders. I have found that individuals who appear to be the most critical are sometimes the most passionate about the church and its future. These are the people who have invested time, emotion, prayers, and finances in your leadership. You need to walk these people through the Rethink Phase.

Work hard to involve the following categories of people in the Rethink Phase:

Board members: Your lay leadership structure and constitutional officers provide you with the organizational authority you need to lead change.

Staff members/volunteers: These people will execute and implement the changes and initiatives that the recalibration process yields.

Influencers: Many people in your church carry significant amounts of influence. You would do well to include their input and buy-in throughout the recalibration process.

Spouses: Few people will know more about your true dreams and deepest hopes than your mate. Your spouse can be a wonderful support, sounding board, and encouragement through your journey.

Critics: Learn to listen to those who disagree with you. Their input, if stewarded properly, can be an invaluable resource for things you don't quite see.

Did that last category surprise you? Do you know who has provided me with some of my most accurate measurements? My critics. They don't always say it with the best attitude, of course. At times, in fact, they have horrible and even hurtful attitudes. But that doesn't mean their observations are false. So listen to their values and passion. Don't get lost in the specific examples. Value their ideas, not necessarily all the words that surround those ideas.

Five Probing and Piercing Questions

In appendix C, I have provided some examples of probing and piercing questions, taken from visionary leaders across the nation. These questions can help a great deal during the Rethink Phase. But here are the five basic probing and piercing questions that catalyze the recalibration process:

1. What is God birthing in your heart as the leader?

As I said in chapter 1, this is the pivotal question to spark a cultural recalibration. Church leaders need to hear from God. They need to know they have a divine assignment at this particular church. You are dealing with people's faith, their lives, and even their finances. You are dealing with sacred tradition and the identity of the church. You have to know that this is God leading you, not merely the latest and coolest idea or fad.

2. How can your church have full Kingdom impact?

Recalibrating a church is not about building your kingdom, but God's. It is not about bodies, budgets, or buildings. It is about reaching deep down inside and asking, "How can my church have full Kingdom impact?" Really wrestle with this question. Don't make this about church growth and bigger buildings. How can you truly have full Kingdom impact on your community and world?

3. What makes you cringe? What bugs you? What frustrates you right now?

You need to get very honest here! For a moment, mentally walk through your Sunday gathering. What makes you privately cringe? What things don't you want to admit? Write them down. How do you really feel about your gatherings? The worship? The ushers? The announcements? The building? The preaching?

Very often, the things that make you cringe are really God's way of speaking to you. Don't get me wrong here—not all cringe-worthy moments are God whispering in your ear. But I do think they indicate a strong direction leaders should consider. (By the way, many leaders need to upgrade their cringe sensitivity, but I guess that's a topic for another book.)

Would you feel comfortable inviting your Starbucks barista to your church? Does anything make you hesitate, even for a moment? What makes you cringe, even for an instant, to invite that neighbor to church? I am not asking, "Are you Mr. or Mrs. Evangelist?" I am asking, "Would you be proud to have your barista or your unchurched neighbor walk into your church?"

I ask this question all the time when teaching recalibration to groups. It's interesting to me that, most of the time, the women in the audience can answer the question more quickly than the men—but they do so slowly and carefully, as if they are walking on thin ice. Perhaps you should privately ask your spouse, "What makes you cringe on a Sunday morning at our church?" Listen carefully! This may be the answer for your church's cultural recalibration.

> **Would you be proud to have your barista or your unchurched neighbor walk into your church?"**

4. If you were able to get over your fear of losing people, what would you stop doing immediately? What would you start doing? Keep doing?

I know this is an impossible question to ask. I don't like losing people. But I've learned that you will lose people. If you decide to be comfortable with the status quo, you will lose people. If you decide to challenge the status quo, you will lose people. I don't like this! It's painful. It's brutal every time I receive an email that announces, "We are leaving because the church isn't deep enough, or friendly enough, or [fill in the blank]."

Here is the brutal reality, however: at the end of day, you will lose far more people by accepting the status quo than by confronting it. It is better to lead and lose some than to coddle and lose all.

5. Where are you? Where are you going? How will you get there?

These three questions represent the beginning point of recalibrating your congregation: your current realities, vision, and vehicle.

Where are you? The facts are your friends. You need to know your current realities. In his recent book *Mission Creep,* Larry Osborne describes the overriding first step for a church to get back on mission. It requires the critical examination of where you are as a church. "If no one realizes that we've drifted," he writes, "everyone thinks we're on target."[32]

Jim Collins, in his well-researched book *Good to Great,* declares that no matter how grim it may be, "You must maintain unwavering faith that you can and will prevail in the end, regardless of the difficulties, AND at the same time have the discipline to confront the most brutal facts of your current reality, whatever they might be.[33] This is the starting point of recalibration.

Where are you going? What vision is God birthing in your heart? Where do you see your church nine months from now? In the next twelve to eighteen months? Five years? What is burning deep down inside you?

How will you get there? The vehicle to recalibrate your church is a Relaunch Initiative. A Relaunch Initiative is a time-bound, well-defined, mission-critical endeavor that serves to recalibrate your church. When you hit the tarmac, you need to date it, define it, and do it.

Let This Get Personal

At times when we say, "You are taking this too personally," we mean it in a negative way. But for a moment, I want to let the future of your church "get personal." It is your personal responsibility and mandate from God to challenge the status quo of your church. Why? If you don't do it, nobody will.

Peter Degon is the pastor of a thirty-six-year-old church, Faith Assembly, located in Lacey, Washington. He became the church's second pastor after its founding pastor served there for more than three decades. At his three-and-a-half year mark, Peter knew the time had come for a cultural recalibration of this established church.

Skeptics told Peter he would lose 40 percent of his people and 30 percent of the finances because he was not the founding pastor of the church. I remember asking Peter, "What is God birthing in your heart for this church?" By his response, it was obvious the church needed some significant cultural changes, including a name change.

> It is your personal responsibility and mandate from God to challenge the status quo of your church.

As he struggled to answer, I followed up with another: "What makes you cringe about your church?" I could tell from a few of his comments that he wanted to discuss the name of the church. "Do you want to stand up one year from now and welcome people to Faith Assembly?" Does the name of your church resonate deeply with you, or make you cringe? This one probing and piercing question was a wake-up call for Peter.

There was a pause.

Followed by a silence.

Then he answered with a resounding "No!" Peter realized in that moment that his biggest fear was losing people and possible disunity over something like a church name.

I could tell Peter wanted to discuss some things burning inside of him, but for whatever reason, he struggled to get them out. But finally the dam broke, and he started listing all things that made him cringe, all the things he thought he needed to rethink and reboot at this church.

It was personal for Peter! He knew, deep down inside, that the church needed a cultural recalibration. It had to make some significant changes. And yet Peter still needed to identify and give clarity to the vision he had.

After working through the principles and practices of recalibration, Peter courageously walked his church through the process of relaunching his church, including a name change and a significant remodel of the building. As a result, his church has grown by 25 percent. Yes, he lost a few people in the process. But the courage to recalibrate was worth it for Peter.

As Peter reflected on the process of confronting the status quo, he told me, "The leadership muscles that challenged me the most were doing an honest assessment, finding the courage to confront the status quo, and asking probing and piercing questions."

For a long time, Peter felt paralyzed by his resistance to rethinking his church and what this would mean for him: "I needed to assess the needed change," he said. "I needed to have the courage to deal with the resistance change would bring. And I needed to define our mission and vision with clarity. These leadership muscles are stronger in me now and will benefit me and the church for decades to come."

Just as Peter let the process get personal for him, so I urge you to let this process get personal for *you!* It's time for you to stop accepting the status quo. It's time for you to get personal about the future of your church:

Get personal about the fact that people in your community are lost and headed toward an eternity without God.

Get personal about the fact that people are sitting in your church in the comfort zone and arguing about things that, at the end of the day, won't really matter.

Get personal about the fact that some people in your community are intrigued and even drawn to Christ, but are afraid that churches won't welcome them.

Get personal about the fact that there are real social needs in your town or city that government can't solve, but that the love of Jesus and the work of the church can.

Coaching Assignments

1. How does your humanity get in the way of facing reality at your church? How does it hinder you from confronting the status quo?

2. In the next three months, how can you get the outside perspective you need? Brainstorm a list of ways. Carve out some money to make it happen.

3. Get away with a few trusted people and ask yourself the five probing and piercing questions in this chapter. This won't be an easy exercise, so take some time for it.

5

PRACTICE #2
CLARIFY NON-NEGOTIABLES:
Preserve the Core, Yet Stimulate Progress

I learned a critical transferable principle about twelve months into my leadership role as the new pastor of New Life church. I started to receive complaints that "Pastor Troy never preaches the Bible." One ruthless email said I preached only "hot topics" in order to draw in large numbers of people.

I saw these critics as completely wrong, of course, and I wanted them to know it. So I emailed back one person, listing every Scripture text I had preached during my first year as lead pastor of New Life. Although I was technically correct, I was also horribly immature. I believe I was more of a brat than a leader.

During this unsettled time, I ran into a transferable leadership principle that literally changed everything at New Life. This one principle has single-handedly helped me recalibrate New Life over and over again. Here's the principle: *The more you change, the more you need to clarify what will never change.*

Let that sink in for a moment.

Your people need to know your non-negotiables. They need to know that you, as a leader, will never weaken the integrity and foundation of the church. It sounds like an oxymoron, but in order for people to follow you as you lead in change, they need to know what you will NEVER change. They need you to be clear on the permanent anchors of your church and your leadership.

"This Is My Pastor!"

New Life went through such a big cultural shift in so many areas that the changes prompted many people to feel as though I were stealing their church. As more and more things began to shift or disappear, people automatically built walls in their minds, thinking, *This thief must be compromising something.*

One Sunday before I started my message, I took a moment to say, "People ask me all the time, 'What do you speak on?' My response is, 'the Bible.' I have sixty-six books to choose from every weekend." New Life always has and always will preach the Bible.

I can't explain what happened that day, but it was as if everyone in the room said, "This is my pastor!" It made them confident that we had a concrete commitment to Scripture that would never falter.

Taking the time to clarify your non-negotiables is especially essential for today, when so many theories and approaches to church inundate the Internet, all of them easily accessible to your people. Many of them fear that their leaders will compromise, sell out, and become like the world. They fear that their leaders will compromise merely to grow the church. Great leaders wisely remove this fear by clearly communicating what will never change. By clarifying non-negotiables, you will:

- Build confidence and trust between the leader and the church. People will follow a leader whom they know has anchoring values that don't change.
- Help your people become more comfortable and adaptive to change.
- Create a culture where people focus on foundational issues.
- Highlight and define the true values of the church.

- Encourage participation in the change process.
- Increase buy-in to the new programs and initiatives.

Preserve the Core, Yet Stimulate Progress

Drucker introduced to the business and organizational world one of the great leadership principles: "Every truly great organization demonstrates the characteristic of preserve the core, yet stimulate progress. The job of the leader is to preserve the core, yet stimulate progress at the same time. If you do one without the other, the organization will become dysfunctional." Drucker insists that all successful organizations and leaders know a few key things on this issue: "They know the difference between what is truly sacred and what is not, between what should never change and what should be always open for change, between 'what we stand for' and 'how we do things.'"[34]

For decades, I have lived my life by the wisdom of a great quotation from F. Scott Fitzgerald, an American novelist and short story writer. His insight changed my life: "The test of a first-rate intelligence is the ability to hold two opposed ideas in mind at the same time, and still retain the ability to function."[35] Preserving the core and stimulating progress may feel like two opposing ideas, but leaders find ways to function within this paradox.

So many leaders get lost in what Collins calls the "Tyranny of the OR," which he says pushes individuals to believe that things must be either A OR B, but not both. "Instead of being oppressed by the 'Tyranny of the OR,'" Collins writes, "highly visionary companies liberate themselves with the 'Genius of the AND'— the ability to embrace both extremes of a number of dimensions at the same time. Instead of choosing between A OR B, they figure out a way to have both A AND B."[36] Many leaders think *preserve the core OR stimulate progress;* in order to successfully recalibrate an established church one needs to think *preserve the core AND stimulate progress.* Preserving the core and stimulating progress may seem like opposing ideas at first glance, but they emphatically are not. They are equal parts of the Recalibration Dance. You have to preserve the core AND stimulate progress, all at the same time. These are not opposing ideologies, but both are essential and must work together.[37]

Returning to Original Specs

When you recalibrate a device, the goal is to return it to the manufacturer's original settings. While massive change is involved in recalibration, its overall purpose of is always to return a church to its original "settings" as purposed by its Manufacturer (in this case, God).

Many established churches have existed for decades without recalibrating, without returning to their original settings. They have drifted so off mission that they care more about music style than worship itself.

How does one clarify the non-negotiables of a church, and then make sure to anchor that church in those non-negotiables? How does a church preserve the core and stimulate progress all at the same time? How does a church leader reset the original settings of the church? Where do you begin? I have identified five things to do during any Rethink Phase of recalibration.

1. Anchor in biblical theology and sound interpretation of Scripture

One of the incredible benefits of doing my doctoral study was the discipline I had to follow to filter all my conclusions about recalibrating a church through Scripture. I built my dissertation's entire second chapter around the biblical and theological foundation of change, recalibration, and mission.

This principle sounds so simple, yet it helps your church navigate change. Take care to remind your church that in middle of a changing culture, biblical theology and sound Scripture will always remain your core. In the middle of change and progress, we have a biblical anchor in our lives that secures us during cultural shifts.

While this is not a theology book nor one that endeavors to help pastors interpret Scripture, I still have to say that we often do ourselves a disservice by declaring some things to be scriptural certainties that, in fact, God in His providence has left unclear. I have seen leaders "ground" things in Scripture that really seemed quite a stretch. Church leaders need to separate the foundational truths of the Bible from their own ideas, perspectives, and opinions.

> In the middle of change and progress, we have a biblical anchor in our lives that secures us during cultural shifts.

I see nothing wrong with communicating your ideas and concepts—in fact, I believe some maybe God-prompted—but leaders who recalibrate well always take care to distinguish between biblical non-negotiables and personal preferences.

At the risk of losing you, allow me to provide a list of some truths I find in the Bible, along with some things not really found there:

- While a concern for modesty is clearly in the Bible, a defined dress code is not.
- Respecting leadership is core in the Bible, but not mindless consent to the leader's every command.
- Drunkenness is forbidden in the Bible, but not moderate alcohol consumption.
- While worship is mandated in Scripture, a particular music style is not.
- Scripture records many prophecies concerning the End Times, but never any prophetic calendar dates.

In my dissertation I studied the famous Jerusalem Council recorded in Acts 15. So many Gentiles were coming to faith in Jesus that the church (still largely Jewish) ran into a heated conflict over circumcision. Think about the tension! Circumcision was a core tradition, a common religious practice and a key cultural ritual of the Jewish nation. To compromise this cultural norm would seem like watering down the teaching of Scripture.

"So what's the big deal?" you ask. Trust me, if you were a thirty-two-year-old male Gentile who just got saved and had never been circumcised, this would be a big deal! The church leaders had to decide right then and there what was non-negotiable and what was open to change.

Into this significant conversation, Peter and James stepped up to clarify the non-negotiables. Peter says in Acts 15:11, "We believe it is through the grace of our Lord Jesus that we are saved, just as they are." Notice how Peter clarifies what was non-negotiable: salvation by faith in Jesus Christ is central, not some religious trapping. James stands up right behind Peter and says in Acts 15:19, "It is my judgment, therefore, that we should not make it difficult for the Gentiles who are turning to God." He further declared that circumcision was not a requirement for salvation—a seismic moment in church history! Peter and James clarified what was non-negotiable and preserved the core, while stimulating progress at the same time.

I am *not* suggesting that leaders shouldn't bother with clear personal standards on issues that the Scriptures leave unclear. For example, I don't personally drink alcohol. My tribe does not consider drinking alcohol an acceptable practice, and I also come from a home destroyed by alcohol. While I have this clear standard in my life, I have to be an honest student of Scripture and accept it as a personal standard and not a scriptural mandate.

Think back to what the early church did. Its leaders isolated the core components of spiritual formation and critical stumbling blocks, and then decided on the most prudent course of action. In that way they managed to preserve the core even while they stimulated progress. The apostles' commands bridged the gap between the ritual sensitivities of Jewish believers and the essence of grace-driven salvation for the Gentiles.

2. Marry the mission, not the methodology

One of the first things a leader has to do is to clearly write out the "why" or the mission of his or her church. I am not talking about some long, drawn-out mission statement that nobody remembers or cares about. I am talking about the overarching mission of the church. It needs to be clear, memorable, and repeatable.

This is so essential when helping people come to grips with cultural change. I learned this lesson firsthand one day when I looked at my calendar and saw a meeting with one of our precious pillars of the church. I have to be honest; I said, "Oh, crap!" I knew she was going to encourage me, yet at the same time remind me about the legacy of the church, the power of the Spirit, and how I needed to remember to never let my head get big. She walked into my office and gently started to talk to me. "Lots of things are changing around here," she said. "Can you share with me your heart and passion?"

I replied, "I would love to!" I took the next thirty minutes to affirm my commitment to Scripture and the Great Commission. I didn't let the conversation get derailed on music style and dress in the auditorium. I told her New Life was about one thing, making disciples of all nations. I told her that I saw a church that would gather on the weekend to worship God and preach the Bible and not get lost in the latest and coolest stuff. I said that I wanted to see everyone develop authentic community, rooted in Scripture, and that the ultimate win is for our people "to be Jesus in the world." I told her, "Here is what will never change: I am passionately committed to the words of Jesus, 'Go and make disciples of all nations.'"

She looked me straight in the eye and said, "I love you, pastor! Thank you for never drifting from the mission. I will follow you! You are my pastor!" Had I drifted off course and started fighting over clothing, ministries, terminology, methods, and other sacred cows, she would have come for a long discussion. But when I focused on the mission, the Scriptures, and the words of Jesus, she immediately went "all in."

Stanley gives leaders some great insights in his book, *Deep & Wide: Creating Churches Unchurched People Love to Attend.* "Marry your mission," he writes. "Date your model. Fall in love with your vision. Stay mildly infatuated with your approach."[38] While we need to be infatuated with our ministry model, we need to be married to our mission. Whenever you talk about change, start by reaffirming the unchanging mission. When you answer questions, talk about the why. When you respond to critics, focus on your non-negotiables.

3. Infuse cultural values

Most established churches began with a deep desire to have some significant Kingdom impact on their world. Over a period of time, however, this value turned into programs and sacred cows. Decades later, people don't talk about the values as much as they discuss the programs. Without an intentional commitment to consistently and continually articulating your church's deep cultural values, people will inevitably emphasize programs and traditions.

> Over the years, I have learned to ignore critics' specific complaints and focus on the deep values that motivate the concern.

When critics confront us, we tend to fight over programs instead of stopping to find agreement on our core values and convictions. Over the years, I have learned to ignore critics' specific complaints and focus on the deep values that motivate the concern.

Infuse the values and convictions that guide every decision and direction you plan to take into every nook and cranny of your church. Jim Kouzes and Barry Posner, authors of *The Leadership Challenge,* are no doubt two of today's premier leadership experts, having spent thirty years studying and researching the subject.

They remind us how values impact any organization:

> Values set the parameters for the hundreds of decisions you make every day, consciously and subconsciously. Values constitute your personal "bottom line." They serve as guides to action. They inform the priorities you set and the decisions you make. They tell you when to say yes and when to say no. They also help you explain the choices you make and why you made them.[39]

I remember walking into "Morning in May," a Saturday event for women at New Life. While it was a great event, it became clear to me that it needed to be recalibrated. When I suggested getting rid of it and dreaming of other ways to create more significant environments for ladies, I got an earful. I stood accused of not believing in women's ministry and not supporting the event. I looked at my critic and said, "I want to see ladies engage in the mission of God and experience deep community. This is what I am stoked about. I am not stoked about any particular program; programs come and go. The heart to see ladies love God and experience deep community is the only value I have here."

Here's how I view the difference between traditions/preferences and deep values/convictions:

Program & Preferences	Values and Convictions
➢ Sunday school	➢ Community & discipleship
➢ Music style	➢ Worshiping God
➢ Midweek kids' programs	➢ Ministry to kids
➢ Women's ministry	➢ Ladies loving God
➢ Sunday night church	➢ Deeper time with God

Carefully delineating between non-negotiables and preferences establishes your credibility as a leader and cements your commitment to the Kingdom values of the organization. Leaders have to know the difference between what is sacred and what is not, between what is core and what is periphery.

4. Recapture your story

One of the greatest yet most overlooked anchors in moving an established church forward is the story and history of your church. Your church has a story. And most churches have a story that provides hints, clues, and even major indicators to their future. You must learn your church's story and then find ways to retell it.

A lot of leaders think the history of their church represents the primary obstacle to effective recalibration, but this is 100 percent false. In fact, the opposite is true; the history of your church is likely where the answer lies to the future of your church.

Read carefully, because I want to say this as clearly as possible. It is simply stupid to minimize or belittle the story and historical roots of the church you lead. While you may not find the answer for your church in its recent years, you might find it in the church's early days. Great leaders leverage the past to build on the future.

When you recalibrate something, the goal is to return it to its original setting. This is why you turn off a computer or router; you are trying to get it back to normal. The story of your church will show you some of the original settings that provide you with themes of the signature of God on that congregation throughout the decades.

Patrick and DeVine describe this beautifully in *Replant*, their work on replanting churches. They argue that history and tradition can become allies in forging a path toward revitalization: "Many times these churches have a valuable gospel DNA; a theological tradition, lost, that needs to be recovered; and a history of God's faithfulness that needs to be retold."[40] They even go further: "In many cases the history of the church and its traditions provide the pastor with the very tools necessary to effect change and renewal."[41]

The greatest tool you have in forging the future of your organization is its own history. What passion started it? What people group or area of town needed you? What spirit and innovation drove its early days? All of these are still nascent in the DNA of your church, waiting to be unlocked and released again.

May 1979: Twenty Dollars and a Handshake

New Life is a story of sacrifice, dreams, and repeatedly recalibrating the mission. Back in 1926, two sisters started the church in their home. The church grew quickly and the two sisters, full of passion and excitement, moved it to a bicycle shop. From that humble beginning, a congregation grew that ultimately built new facilities, changed the name of the church a few times, and started some innovative ministries that reached the community. It also sacrificed deeply. To read the entire New Life story, you can visit my website at *www.recalibrategroup.com/resources*.

Great leaders leverage the past to build on the future.

By 1979, the church had experienced some incredible momentum under the leadership of Pastor John Tappero. The board decided to expand at their location in downtown Renton, developing new plans to fill in the courtyard area and add more space. Still located in the church archives, the plans indicate that they included more nursery space, classrooms, and more office space for the pastor.

In a board meeting on April 21, 1979, they got ready to approve the plans to build again. Then one of the board members, Darrell Jones, raised his hand and said, "We are not thinking big enough. Before we build more classrooms and the nursery in the courtyard, shouldn't we pause and take a look at our growth over the last decade and ask if this building can facilitate future growth?"

At first, Pastor Tappero, at the age of sixty-four, felt very reluctant about this proposal. The board, however, had several young leaders from the ages of twenty-six to forty who saw the future and potential of this church. Pastor Tappero fondly called these board members the "Young Turks," meaning they pushed the envelope of growth and evangelism. According to Pastor Tappero, this board had a "willingness to try new ideas" and its members "anticipated growth."

Pastor Tappero gave these Young Turks permission to look for new land. In May of 1979, Darrell Jones, Dean Bitney (a local realtor who belonged to the church), and Frank Huebner (associate pastor) found a piece of property on Maple Valley Highway. At this point in time, this location seemed way out in the farmlands and outside of anyone's imagination for growth. Regardless, the three men knocked on the door of a local Renton doctor, Dr. Heilpern, who owned the property. Bitney knew that although Dr. Heilpern had the property on the market earlier that year, he had taken if off because he did not want to sell his homestead to a housing development.

After a couple hours of conversation, the men agreed on an asking price of $855,000 for fifty-seven acres of land and the house on the property.[42] With a handshake, these church members agreed in principle to buy the property from Dr. Heilpern for the stipulated price. When Dr. Heilpern asked about earnest money, Darrell Jones reached into his pocket and said, "Will twenty dollars do?" With another handshake, Dr. Heilpern accepted twenty dollars as earnest money. In July of 1979, Darrell Jones updated the board on the negotiations with Dr. Heilpern, explaining the asking price would be $855,000 or $15,000 per acre.

Every weekend when I walk into New Life, I see Darrell Jones. He reminds me of the story of New Life. This story is one of sacrifice and commitment. By the way, eight of the twelve Young Turks still go to New Life. Three have passed away; one attends a nearby church.

Your church has a story! Go back far enough to uncover it. Someone planted that church. Someone believed God for great things. Someone paid a great price. They didn't pay this price to fight about programs, music style, or doctrine. They paid the price of change to reach their area for Christ.

5. Be yourself

One of the non-negotiables you need to anchor into your own soul is getting comfortable in your own skin. Stop trying to be someone you are not! I don't mean you should use this as an excuse to allow your church to get ingrown, become stagnant, and drift off mission. But the worst thing you can do is try to be a leader you are not.

The best-selling leadership classic *Discover Your True North* by Bill George enables you to become an authentic leader by discovering your True North, or as I like to say, discovering your own voice. As a result of first-person interviews with leaders of all ages, various industries and different cultures, George has concluded, "The reality is that no one can be authentic by trying to be like someone else. You can learn from others' experiences, but you cannot be successful trying to be like them. People will trust you only when you are genuine and authentic."[43]

The Legacy of Dr. Rick Ross

Dr. Rick Ross is my pastor and spiritual father. I met him in 1989, right before I graduated from Northwest University. He hired me as the youth pastor of the church I currently pastor. For the last twenty-six-plus years, he has taught me more than any single human being. I sat in the front row, watching him recalibrate New Life with grace and courage. He was the one who moved our congregation from downtown Renton to its current location. Without his courageous leadership, New Life would not be the church it is today. He is the one who modeled for me how to recalibrate established churches and how each church has a story that needs to be captured and retold. I recently watched him dance with his daughter, Karissa, at her wedding. I will say he is not much of a dancer—but he knows the Recalibration Dance better than any person I know.

One thing Dr. Ross taught me has shaped my leadership to this day, a principle we've considered earlier: preserve the core, yet stimulate progress. He never put it like that, but he certainly modeled it over the years. I can still hear Dr. Ross say to me, with the animated cadence only he has:

"You have to be careful not to water down the gospel."

"Don't change for the sake of change."

"Keep the main thing the main thing."

I watched Dr. Ross reaffirm the core values of New Life, anchor all changes in Scripture, recapture the church's story, and infuse strong cultural values into the DNA of the church.

Preserve the core, yet stimulate progress. If you miss this one transferable principle, you will ultimately hurt not only your church, but will also compromise the very character and nature of the church.

Coaching Assignments

1. Take some time to identify three to five core passages of the Bible that have and will continue to shape the way you lead your church. Write them down. Share them with your board, staff, and key people in your church.

2. Clearly identify the mission and core values of your church. Ground this in Scripture. Write them down. Preach on them. Talk about them.

3. Read the story of your church. What does the story teach you? What are some values and overall signature characteristics of your church?

6

PRACTICE #3
THINK MISSION CRITICAL:
Change Only What You Have to Change

M any pastors and leaders feel paralyzed. They have no idea where to begin. I often hear one common frustration from pastors, boards, spouses, and church teams: "Will we ever really make any of these changes? I am tired of all the talking and discussion . . . let's *do* something!"

While working with one church, I heard one team member blurt out, "We have been talking about these kinds of changes for way too long." Even the pastor's own wife asked, "Are we really going to do this? I am tired of talking about all this change and doing nothing!"

As I dug deeper into the heart of this pastor, I recognized the problem: he thought he needed to make all the changes at once, or make none of them at all.

> You need to focus on the changes that will move your congregation forward, not all the merely important things on your radar.

This idea had paralyzed him for years. It didn't help that he also feared losing people and wondered whether he'd be able to hang on to his job.

"You don't have to make all the changes now," I told him, "change only what you have to change. You need to focus on the changes that will move your congregation forward, not all the merely important things on your radar."

At first he looked puzzled and even confused, so I continued. "You don't have the leadership credibility to make all the changes in your heart," I said, "and you don't have the money. But what's more important is that not all the changes are mission critical. Not all these changes will move your church forward. Quite the opposite—you will only frustrate your people instead of moving the church forward."

Here's the transferable principle: *Identify the mission-critical changes that will move your church forward, distinguishing them from what is merely important.*

Don't Get Paralyzed

During the Rethink Phase, all types of ideas, concepts, changes, and directions for the future will get passionately discussed and debated. Some comments will be tough to hear. Some observations will get overstated and over-personalized. It will feel overwhelming to rethink your church. It will feel deeply personal. And it will be very easy to get paralyzed by all the gut-wrenching ideas and concepts thrown around.

But remember that a Relaunch Initiative is a time-bound, well-defined, mission-critical initiative that serves as a catalyst to recalibrate your church. Not all changes are mission critical. Not all changes will serve as a catalyst to recalibrate the church. Changes must be mission critical, or they will only frustrate the church and eat away at the pastor's credibility and the church's momentum.

Mission-critical changes are intentional alterations that move the congregation forward, not merely changes for the sake of change. They require a leader to focus his or her energy on the few changes or behaviors that will make a world of difference.

Recalibration requires leaders to engage in mission-critical thinking instead of reacting impulsively to all the needs they see around them. Leaders must think of the changes that will move the congregation significantly forward.

Often, when people study the lives of great leaders, they get the impression that these leaders change everything all at once. We hear voices in our head saying, "If *you* were a courageous leader, you would make all these changes *right now.*"

Do you know what? Those voices are wrong. They lie. I don't call this being a courageous leader; I call it being stupid.

This is particularly true when leading an established church. Many traditions, programs, and systems are deeply rooted in the culture of the church. When you begin to confront the status quo, you will find that many things hinder the church from moving forward. The list seems endless and can feel overwhelming. It may feel as though you need to tackle everything at once—but if you attempt to change everything in a single bound . . .

> Not all changes will serve as a catalyst to recalibrate the church

- You will lose credibility and kill the organization.
- You will confuse your people.
- You will waste leadership capital where you don't have to waste it.
- You will waste emotional bandwidth on issues and things that simply don't merit such attention.

The authors of *The 4 Disciplines of Execution* discuss the difficult choices a leader must make during a change initiative: "To succeed, you must be willing to make the hard choices that separate what is wildly important from all the many other merely important goals on your radar."[44] In other words, you can't accomplish all your goals overnight. Good leaders understand what is merely important versus what is mission critical. You must know what will move your organization forward and what will have little to no impact.

According to the authors of *Influencer*, leaders must find a handful of key behaviors that will facilitate leading change: "Success relies on the capacity to systematically create rapid, profound, and sustainable changes in a handful of key behaviors."[45] Relaunch Initiatives create rapid, profound, and sustainable changes in mission-critical areas that will move the congregation significantly forward. Eventually, these changes will spark a chain reaction and contribute to the tipping point of the congregation, ultimately relaunching the church and infusing new DNA into its life.

Four Quadrants of Change

At this point, you must ask four key leadership questions: What changes do I make now, and which ones are better left for later? How fast will we move? What are the merely important decisions that need to be put on the back burner for now? How do I decide exactly what changes to make?

In order to effectively answer these questions, you have to understand that not all changes are the same. It helps to recognize four types of changes:

Mission-critical: You must address these changes in a specific, time-bound way in order to move the mission forward. If these changes are not made, the congregation simply will not achieve full Kingdom impact and will put its future in jeopardy.

Merely important: You don't need to address these changes immediately, unless they will give the leader credibility for other, more important changes. A leader acknowledges these changes but may wisely put them on the back burner and wait for a more appropriate time to make them.

Load bearing: These kinds of changes alter the culture. You ask people to change their accepted behaviors and beliefs, along with the deep-seated "whys" of a church or organization.

Non-load bearing: These kinds of changes, consistent with your culture, provoke minimal negative responses.

It is easy to cop out and say that since people resist change, there is no hope for your church or organization. While many people do indeed resist change, the core issue is a cultural problem, not resistance to change itself. People tend to resist *cultural* change, not *all* change.

When remodeling an old home, for example, you have to distinguish between load-bearing walls and non-load-bearing walls (partition walls or floating walls, as my contractor likes to call them). Load bearing walls are capable of supporting a structural load in addition to their own weight and are essential to maintaining the structural integrity of a house. A non-load-bearing wall, by contrast, is subject only to its own weight and configuration.

> People tend to resist cultural change, not all change.

While all walls can be taken down during a remodel, a wise contractor knows the difference in difficulty between removing a partition wall and a load bearing wall.

Or more simply put, some changes are easier than others. So how do you tell the difference between a load-bearing wall and a non-load bearing wall? Not an easy question to answer. However, you can consider a few definite indicators that suggest you may be dealing with a load bearing wall:

- How long has the ministry (or system) been around? The longer it has been at the church, the more likely it is a load bearing wall.

- Who started the ministry? If the former pastor or some highly influential person in the congregation started the program, the more likely it is a load-bearing wall.
- Will someone lose his or her paying job or place of influence in the church? If so, the more likely it is a load-bearing wall.
- Is this ministry connected to people's life-changing experience with God? The greater the emotional attachment, the more likely it is a load-bearing wall.
- How much money has been spent on this ministry or environment? The more money that has been invested, the more likely it is a load-bearing wall.

The following diagram illustrates how these four types of change intersect with each other and form what I call the "Four Quadrants of Change."

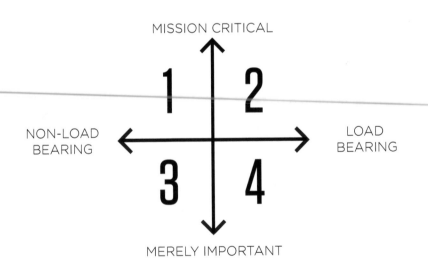

These quadrants provide leaders with some insight into when and how to approach changes within their congregation.

1. Mission-critical, non-load-bearing changes

Start here when it comes to change. Get quick wins. Celebrate those wins. Make the changes that will move the mission forward but not cause a cultural clash. These changes need to be made quickly and efficiently, but be careful, because even non-load-bearing changes can cause discomfort. Still, the future of your church hangs in the balance if you don't make these changes.

These quick wins may include things like changing the assimilation process, a relatively inexpensive remodel of a ministry room, painting some walls, cleaning up the bathrooms, or simply making fewer announcements. Many pastors have discovered a quick win in working to become a better preacher. Long sermons that feel irrelevant to a congregation may be a load-bearing wall in the pastor's life, but no congregation will push back against someone stepping up his preaching game.

2. Mission-critical, load-bearing changes

Every leader should focus on these types of changes. Such changes will make a world of difference for your congregation, but they must be carefully made. By far, these are the most difficult changes to make.

When you take down a load-bearing wall, you have to create a supporting system to hold up the house while the old walls come down. It's expensive. It takes time. But it must be done! If you lack the courage and vision to lead your church in these kinds of changes, you put the future of your church in jeopardy. This is where you need to realign the culture (discussed in detail in part 3).

In many churches, this may include changes to worship style, the overall culture of Sundays, staff changes, attitudes toward outsiders, long services, power struggles with the board, expending resources on programs and events that no longer work, cluttered calendars, strange expressions of the Holy Spirit, or overuse of religious language incomprehensible to outsiders.

3. Merely important, non-load-bearing changes

The timing of changes in this category depends on finances, timing, and vision. Your church will easily accept these changes, which may even provide the leader with some quick wins. If your church has stagnated, make as many changes as possible in quadrants 1 and 3.

Examples of changes in this category may be as simple as fresh paint, new landscaping, added signage throughout the building, updated technology or even modifying the order of the service.

Quickly make these non-load-bearing changes if you have the finances and emotional bandwidth. By doing so, you begin to create a culture where change is normal: a culture of recalibration.

4. Merely important, load-bearing changes

You can and should put these changes on the back burner. You will eventually have the emotional bandwidth to get to them, but if they aren't hurting your mission-critical momentum, don't get lost on them. Don't waste your emotional energy and leadership capital by trying to deal with them immediately.

Consider just a few of the things that I consider quadrant 4 changes at New Life. These are load-bearing changes but not mission critical.

- Boys' and girls' midweek programs. It took me 10 years before I made this change at New Life.
- Constitution and bylaws. I feel embarrassed to admit this, but we still need to update our constitution and bylaws.
- Membership process: Our membership process still makes me cringe. One day, we will recalibrate this entire process! For now, we haven't deemed the issue mission critical to the future of New Life.

A classic example for New Life was our adult Sunday school program. When I started, we had ten classes; however, I knew that with our children's ministry growing, we would need more space for the kids. Although this was a load-bearing wall at New Life, we had to move slowly to make this change. Today, we have just one adult Sunday school class.

To Change or Not to Change?

Find a whiteboard and write down all the things that make you cringe as a staff and board. Make sure you involve your spouse in this. After you get the long list of changes, put them into one of the four change quadrants.

> Wise leaders recognize that the wisest thing to do, at times, is simply to wait until the culture shifts.

Now, where do you start? Think mission critical! Use all your energy and time to focus on mission-critical changes, not merely important ones.

A certain leadership paradox occurs when you deal with load-bearing changes and non-load-bearing changes. Once you start infusing new culture into your church, many things that the church once treated as cultural changes (load-bearing) can, over a period of time, become non-load-bearing changes.

I remember the first time I suggested to the board that New Life cancel our senior high Sunday school class. I felt so excited! I wanted all our senior high students to serve at the church and attend one service. I had all kinds of great reasons for the change.

My board flatly rejected the idea. I ran smack into the middle of a cultural change, a load-bearing wall. I had no idea that my suggestion would create so much tension. I quickly recognized it as a cultural shift not worth fighting for (at the moment). High school Sunday school, I realized, wasn't mission critical for me. So I paused and didn't force it.

Three years later, in another board meeting, the subject came up again. This time, in a casual conversation, our board said, "With all the groups meeting throughout the week, why keep the senior high Sunday school class? It would be better for them to serve and attend a service."

What had happened? After three years of cultural realignment and changing the cultural language of the church, what had once been a load-bearing wall, a divisive power struggle, had become a partition wall easily taken down. Wise leaders recognize that the wisest thing to do, at times, is simply to wait until the culture shifts.

Think Mission Critical

Leaders need to create a clear definition of "mission critical" for their organizations. This is the starting point and perhaps the most difficult part of recalibrating an established church. When coaching leaders, I always ask, "What is mission critical for your church or organization? How do you define it?" The answer will significantly shape what you focus on now and what you can put on the back burner.

Every leader has to define for his or her own situation what is mission critical and what is merely important. Your decisions in this area may be the single most important decisions you ever make as a leader.

Not to put on the pressure, but mission-critical changes are also very difficult to determine. Once you define what mission critical means for you, however, you must engage all your leadership capital, resources, and emotional bandwidth to make these changes happen.

The following three key questions can help any leader define an organization's mission-critical changes:

1. What changes will move the mission forward?

Don't get lost in making changes and generating activities that don't move the congregation and mission forward. You have nothing to prove. A merely important change may seem "cool," but cool is not your goal. Your goal is to advance the Kingdom of God in your community through your church. Focus your energy and efforts on changes that will make significant contributions to that mission.

The authors of *Influencer* speak directly to where leaders need to put their energy: "Don't put precious energy into strategies that rapidly propel you in the wrong direction."[46] This is so big! No success is more dangerous than success in the wrong direction, because this will lead to a deceptively healthy church, a false sense of fulfillment, and eventually the erosion of your Kingdom impact. I meet leaders all the time who are hard at work on changes that will never move the mission forward. That's why they lose credibility.

2. What changes will give your congregation the greatest impact?

"What changes will yield the greatest impact" is a totally different question than "what change is most important?" Mission-critical changes focus on the greatest impact. These changes represent the decisions that most effectively leverage resources, mobilize volunteers, and connect to the greater community.

The authors of *The 4 Disciplines of Execution* define a vital question that leaders must ask themselves when leading times of change. The question is not, "What is most important?" but rather, "If every other area of our operation remained at its current level of performance, what is the one area where change would have the greatest impact?" This question changes the way you think and lets you clearly identify the focus that would make all the difference.[47]

Osborne echoes the same conviction in his book *Innovation's Dirty Little Secret*. He says that innovators don't "try to fix everything that's broken or improve things that aren't running perfectly. Instead, they focus on fixing the things that will make the biggest difference."[48] If the change you're considering won't make the biggest difference in the next season for your church, then it's not a mission-critical change.

Effective leaders consistently look for the two to three mission-critical changes in an organization that will create the greatest impact. Most avalanches result not from a sudden combination of sizable shifts, but from the gradual buildup of pressure due to small changes in the distribution of the snow. In a similar way, a few key changes, combined with the weight and momentum of progress, can cause seismic change in your organization.

> Leaders have to get beyond "I hope this will happen" to "This will happen by this precise date."

The authors of *Influencer* claim that it takes only a few changes to create a cascade of benefits: "Master influencers know that it takes only a few behaviors to create big changes in the results they care about. To do so, they look vigilantly for one or two actions that create a cascade of change."[49]

Focus on a few behaviors to cultivate momentum and the catalytic tipping points in your church. Focus on the mission-critical changes that will give you the greatest impact. These are the changes need to be on the front burner; merely important ones can be on the back burner for now.

3. What changes can you actually achieve during your Relaunch Initiative?

Honestly ask yourself, "What changes can I actually achieve during this time-bound, well-defined, mission-critical Relaunch Initiative?"

By its very nature, the phrase "time-bound" implies that you can't accomplish everything within a specified time frame. Yes, leaders need to stretch themselves and think big. But at some point, they also must have the ability to think in terms of what they can actually accomplish in a limited time frame.

What mission-critical changes do you want to lead in your church over the next nine months? Date it. Define it. Do it. Everything else belongs on the back burner. Leaders have to get beyond "I hope this will happen" to "This *will* happen by this precise date."

When answering this question, leaders need to consider several current realities:

- Financial implications
- Emotional bandwidth
- Personal life expectations
- Credibility issues within the church

Once you know the answer, give yourself permission to put everything else on the back burner. Write down the mission-critical changes—the ones you can accomplish in the time frame you established—and pour all your energy and effort into achieving them.

The Mission-Critical Pieces of My Own Journey

While I have no interest in telling you how to do church, I know that everyday illustrations can help leaders to better understand these concepts and form a beginning point to apply them. So let me return briefly to my first year of leading New Life.

In a word, it was painful. I was all of thirty-six years old and had all types of changes stirring in my heart. I quickly found myself in way over my head. I was trying to navigate being a new pastor, hiring staff (about which I had no clue), and making changes that I had dreamed about for years. Inevitably, I made a lot of unfortunate mistakes.

To my credit, I knew that I needed a mission statement, core values, and even a ministry model. But I didn't know that I also had to clearly define the mission-critical changes required to move the church forward.

I wish someone had told me that first year that I needed to focus on mission-critical changes only and put the merely important changes on the back burner! That single piece of advice would have saved me many sleepless nights. Unfortunately, it took me about two years to make the discovery on my own. Only then did I stop trying to make all the changes and started focusing my changes on three mission-critical areas.

I finally realized that if New Life was going to achieve its full Kingdom impact, we had to focus on the following mission-critical ministries: Sundays, children, and groups. At New Life, we defined mission-critical changes as "anything that negatively impacts or drains energy from Sundays, kids, or life groups." That decision largely directed my first five years of leadership. Later on, we added two more mission-critical ministries, local & global missions, and youth ministry.

At New Life, we determined that something was mission critical if the issue in question hindered people from inviting others to church or stopped people from sticking to the church. That single principle changed everything at New Life. Everything else became a secondary consideration, a back burner conversation. We would deal with them later.

Sounds simple, doesn't it? Unfortunately, it's not. Not even close.

I have spent a dozen years of my life on these mission-critical ministries of New Life, directing all our resources to these three environments:

Sundays. This includes everything that happens from the street to the seat, from the first handshake to the last amen. Sundays are the central nervous system of New Life; from here, everything flows and returns. Sundays have the greatest impact over the largest number of people at a single time.

Children's ministry. We chose to target young families in the Pacific Northwest. It seemed clear to me that young families bring their kids to church with them, and so children's ministry became mission critical to moving New Life forward. This felt especially paradoxical to me, because I had given fifteen years of my life to youth ministry. But I knew that if New Life were to achieve its full Kingdom impact, it would have to put all of its energy and effort into building a world-class children's ministry.

Groups. I didn't want New Life to become simply about larger gatherings. At the heart of the church is discipleship. I knew that if I limited our discipleship method to Sunday school, this would limit our kids' ministry for space and workers. It would also limit people to stuffy rooms that didn't create the kind of community and relationships that foster spiritual depth and health. So we made groups mission critical over Sunday school.

I gave myself permission to put on the back burner merely important changes that I simply didn't have bandwidth to force or the leadership capital to change. People who have heard the New Life story sometimes get the idea that I came in and made all these sweeping changes with one stroke of the pen. Hardly! I chose the mission-critical changes and moved other priorities and preferences (even my own) to the back burner.

> The greatest piece of advice I can give leaders who want to recalibrate an established church is this: *start with Sundays.*

Start with Sundays

The greatest piece of advice I can give leaders who want to recalibrate an established church is this: *start with Sundays.*

Put everything else on the back burner. I believe Sunday is the most mission-critical environment you have. If you are doing your first recalibration, I encourage you to focus on Sunday. Most leaders tend to underestimate the power of the Sunday gathering for embedding the mission, creating culture, and casting vision to the congregation. At the same time, they overestimate the importance of peripheral programs to communicate the vision of the church.

Why is Sunday so important?

- Sunday impacts the church's soul and culture.
- Sunday happens every 165 hours.

- Sunday is the day you model to the church what you believe and what is most important to you.
- Sundays provide a platform to engage new people with the vision of the church.
- Sunday is an opportunity to re-educate longtime members on the church's mission.

Recalibrating our Sunday mornings took time. Consider two of the most mission critical changes we made to recalibrate our Sunday gatherings:

First, on March 21, 2004, we started a new Sunday noon service called "The Well" that allowed me to discover and experiment with how to do church. We did not conceive of it as a "contemporary service," but in fact, it was my way of learning and experimenting with how I wanted to lead New Life into the future. Today, New Life mirrors this service. We finally eliminated the Well after the experimental style became a cultural norm.

Second, on August 15, 2004, we started a traditional service called Softer Sundays. This service featured timeless music and hymns, and congregants watched the message on a large-screen TV, utilizing a broadcast-quality DVR player.

Both of these moves contributed greatly to what New Life has become. In the almost twelve years since their launch, they've helped redefine the DNA of our church and set us up for further growth.

Today, we have ten Sunday gatherings on three campuses, all reflecting the culture of these early decisions. We still do Softer Sundays, having found it the key to honoring the spiritual giants of the past while infusing new cultural DNA into the heart of the church.

None of this would have happened if I had focused on merely important changes at New Life. Instead, I focused on a few mission-critical initiatives that moved our church forward . . . and so transformed the culture of New Life.

Game On!

This is the time for real action. This is the time to date it, define it, and do it. It is the time to carefully weigh your options and make some key decisions.

Accept that any decision (or lack of one) will carry its own consequences. Embrace them. In doing so, you will create the necessary tension points to move your church forward into its next great season.

The purpose of the Rethink Phase is to prepare for action, not for more talk. In the words of Elvis Presley: "A little less conversation, a little more action, please."

The authors of *The 4 Disciplines of Execution* describe what happens in teams that do this:

> When a team moves from having a dozen we-really-hope goals to one or two no-matter-what goals, the effect on morale is dramatic. It's as though a switch exists in every team member's head called 'Game on!' If you can throw that switch, you have laid the foundation for extraordinary execution. When President Kennedy said to the moon and back by the end of the decade, he threw that switch.[50]

What mission-critical changes will get your staff up in the morning to work? Which ones will make a world of difference? What changes, if made, will start to recalibrate the culture of your church? What changes will cause your board, staff, and congregation to say "Game on! Let's do this"?

Write them down!

Set the date!

Let's relaunch your church.

Coaching Assignments

1. Sit down with your staff and write down all the things that make you cringe as a team. After you finish this list, put all the changes into one of the Four Quadrants of Change:

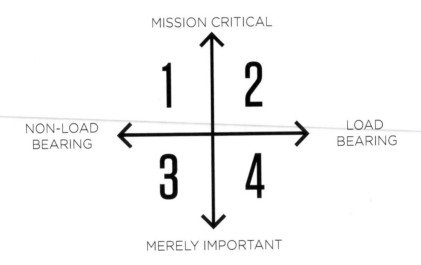

2. Take some time to define the term "mission critical" at your church. How would you define this term in the context of your congregation?

3. What mission-critical changes do you need to make in the next nine months? What are some merely important changes that you can put on the back burner?

Part Three

THE REALIGN PHASE:
INFUSE NEW CULTURAL DNA INTO YOUR CHURCH

Why do most church revitalizations fail? It's a dangerous question with a simple answer: They fail because real change never seeps into the cultural fabric of the church.

Infusing new cultural DNA into your congregation is by far the most complicated and time-consuming part of developing a continuous culture of recalibration. But until the change is aligned and seeps into your culture, there will be no lasting and meaningful change. No change initiative will stick if it doesn't seep deeply into the cultural roots of your church.

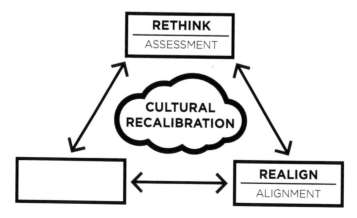

In part 3, we'll consider the fatal attraction of most churches and discuss three more of the nine crucial leadership practices that I refer to as Realign Practices:

- *Practice #4* | Establish a Cultural Lexicon:
  Language Creates Culture
- *Practice #5* | Celebrate Short-Term Wins:
  Tangible Examples of the New Cultural Norm
- *Practice #6* | Cast Clear Vision:
  The Catalyst for Meaningful and Lasting Change

Realigning culture requires leaders to learn skills that simply were never taught to them at Bible college, seminary, or training conferences. In this section, I will ask you to stretch yourself beyond belief. You *have* to realign the church's culture. Making cosmetic changes may feel exciting, but such changes will never enable your church to reach its full Kingdom impact.

7

CULTURAL MISALIGNMENT:
A Church's Fatal Attraction

A few years ago, the A&E Network created a television documentary series that explored a fascinating and disturbing mental disorder. *Hoarders* focused on compulsive hoarding, an anxiety disorder characterized by "a pattern of behavior that is characterized by excessive acquisition and an inability or unwillingness to discard large quantities of objects that cover the living areas of the home and cause significant distress or impairment."[51]

Each week, viewers found themselves in the homes of men and women who comforted themselves or coped through the persistent collection of materials, items, and even animals. These homes often looked quite normal on the outside—but on the inside, cameras recorded rooms stacked to the roof with garbage, collectible items, or old memorabilia. The accumulated items created fire hazards, collapsing piles of garbage, and other serious health dangers.

Most of us never realize we're gathering so much junk; we simply collect and collect until the buildup overwhelms us. We confuse what we want with what we need, and what we need with what we already have.

Unfortunately, many churches find themselves in a similar

predicament. Except rather than collecting porcelain dolls, cats, or old newspapers, they collect programs, ministries, and plans. They cram as much as possible into the church calendar and overwhelm parishioners with an avalanche of activities and promotions.

Compulsive hoarding creates a dysfunctional church environment. Most churches are misaligned simply because they do too much. They're too busy. Too many nights out. Too many announcements. Too many programs. We spend so much time hoarding ministries and clutter that we lack focus, clarity, and intentionality. Our culture is misaligned.

The fatal attraction of deceptively healthy churches is that they say yes to everything. They try to please everybody and end up reaching nobody. The fatal attraction of established churches is clutter, busyness, and a "silo mentality" that leads to a messy, confusing, misaligned organization.

Is Your Church Misaligned?

Consider a few telltale signs that your church is misaligned. Do you see any of the following signs in your church?

- An exhausted staff
- Announcements that make you cringe
- A ministry model that requires people to be at the church too much
- Spending more money on productions than on mission-critical ministries
- Everyone competing for finances and facilities
- A stuffed calendar with no margins
- Every department has a different mission statement and values
- Departments compete for volunteers and workers
- Your church isn't growing

If you recognize two or more of these symptoms in your church, then almost certainly you're suffering from some degree of misalignment. For your church to move forward, you have to get it aligned.

What Is Cultural Alignment?

We might define cultural alignment in a church or ministry organization like this: "Arranging the mission, ministry model, systems, staff, and ministries so that they all work together, heading in the same direction."

To align things means to arrange them in a straight line. In most arenas of life, we love alignment! Proper alignment in our car means the vehicle is running smoothly, safely and efficiently. When life comes together favorably, some people say, "The stars have aligned." In geometry, we all learned that the shortest distance between two points is a straight line. Efficiency and good results come from alignment.

When I think of cultural alignment, I automatically think of the way houses are designed. If you were to walk into my historic house, you would find a Craftsman-style front porch, charming and full of character. Dead center of the porch, you'd see a red door that invites people to enter. An entryway gets you into the house. Once inside, you'd notice hardwood floors, wainscoting, and family pictures, everything working together to create a warm, welcoming entrance. A family room is located off the kitchen, with another room for people to sit together or watch TV. As you walk through the house, various hallways and stairs connect you to bathrooms, bedrooms, and the kitchen.

The architect aligned the house to work as a unit, arranging it to eliminate competing systems. All the rooms and environments are arranged and positioned in ways that create a comfortable living space for our family.

Now think about your church. Do visitors know how to enter the front door? Once they enter, are there obvious and strategic ways to find a place where the guest can get questions answered? Can guests expect to be welcomed by people who look friendly and inviting?

Most churches put all their furniture in the entryway, along with banners for fundraisers, sign-ups for ministries, and tables for books and resources. That would be like entering my house and finding a refrigerator, stove, toilet, and the master bed, right there in the entry. We need all these things in our house, but placed more sensibly. All these things need to be aligned correctly. The refrigerator is therefore in the kitchen, by the sink. The master bed is upstairs, by a dresser and the walk-in closet. The toilet is in the bathroom.

Now think about how many church programs are organized: People show up to church on Sunday morning. They attend an adult Sunday school class. They come back on Sunday night. Don't forget Wednesday night and midweek programs! If you are really spiritual, you may throw in a committee meeting or two. Busy. Busy. Busy.

We used to do pretty much all of these things. At every meeting, we sang a few songs, received an offering (can't miss this), listened to never-ending announcements, and heard a long sermon.

Where does that tend to leave people today? Many leave dissatisfied, never empowered to grow passionately in their love for God and people. You must start to think of your church as traveling along a different trajectory. Ask yourself some crucial questions:

- Are the mission, core values, ministry model, vision, and programs of your church in perfect sync, flowing effortlessly across age groups and departments?
- Does everything from the parking lot to the final prayer make sense in relationship to each other? Or do some things fight against other things?
- Do your departments compete for people, money, and space?
- Can everyone on your leadership or influencing team share your vision and mission, using the same words?

Again, think of your car. When everything is in alignment, you never notice it. The transmission, chassis, and axle all interact seamlessly, giving you a smooth ride. Over time, however, the alignment of your car naturally starts to degrade. You may not feel it at first, or you may ignore the warning signs, but soon the problem will result in an uncomfortable ride and eventually a broken vehicle. When something is out of alignment, it costs more to run because it runs less efficiently.

Most churches and organizations are ineffective not because they are irrelevant, but because they are out of alignment. Aligning your church so that all the pieces, departments, staff, structures, and programs work together seamlessly is the greatest challenge of church leadership. Church practices that don't align with the church's mission waste more money, energy, and emotional bandwidth than any other issue.

> Most churches and organizations are ineffective not because they are irrelevant, but because they are out of alignment.

If you don't align your church, all the Relaunch Initiatives and mission-critical changes in the world will never move your church forward. When you work to align your church, however, it will run more smoothly, staff will become more effective, and you will be able to reach more people for Christ.

What Causes Misalignment?

Congregational misalignment occurs when ministries, programs, and systems work as silos, competing against each other for the resources of the organization and ultimately leaving people busy but not on mission with the church. You might use words and phrases like "discombobulated," "out of whack," or just plain "broken" to describe this dysfunctional condition.

Many things can cause your church or organization to get out of alignment. The fact is, the longer it has been around, the more likely it is out of alignment. Ponder several common issues that fight against alignment in your church.

Seven-day church. Frankly, we have been taught (and modeled) quite the opposite of cultural alignment. The seven-day church life has been taught to us as the gold standard. The unintended consequence of this approach is the thinking that the busier the church, the better. We all have known churches that boast of their long list of disconnected ministries.

Find a need and fill it. I was raised on the ministry philosophy, "Find a need and fill it." While this feels good to say, it has hurt the church. It has caused church calendars to get too full, encouraged staff people to compete over limited resources and announcement time, and ultimately drained churches to the core. We end up doing so many things poorly.

Ministry and program clutter. The biggest reason churches and organizations get out of cultural alignment is what I call "clutter." Over time, churches add and accumulate traditions, ministries, and programs . . . and never get rid of any of them. Clutter will throw your church into misalignment faster than anything! Too many churches start ministries without ever ending any of them.

> The biggest reason churches and organizations get out of cultural alignment is what I call "clutter."

Church lens. Everyone has a church lens. It doesn't matter if you were raised in church or don't even like church; everyone has a church lens. Every person sitting in your pews believes he or she knows church and the way it should be. This is one big reason why the 350,000 churches across America are misaligned. What makes this worse is that we have been taught to provide ministry opportunities for everyone's church lens. While that may sound good in theory, in fact, all these programs, styles, and initiatives simply don't fit together.

Sacred cows. The idea of a sacred cow comes from a popular (although not entirely accurate) understanding of Hindu culture, in which cows are so greatly revered that they cannot be hurt or killed. Sacred cows in your church or organization are the things everyone considers untouchable or sacrosanct.

Sacred cows serve no real mission purpose and unnecessarily drain volunteers and resources. A sacred cow could be a church library that no one uses (but the space could make a nice toddler's nursery). A sacred cow might be the space on the wall where the founding pastor's portrait hangs (that could instead be used to highlight local missions and service projects). It might be that Sunday night service where people gather for "deeper" experiences with God (but in fact has become an exercise in self-congratulation and self-serving performance). Sacred cows cost the church more than they are worth, whether in money, time, or energy.

Cultural Alignment Starts Here

Cultural alignment is very difficult and could cost you more than any other single change you will make. Like remodeling, it will take longer than you think and cost you more than you were planning.

- It will force you to take a hard look at your church budget.
- It will force you to see your current and future staff in a different way.
- It will force you to view your communication strategy from a holistic perspective.
- It will force you to look at every department and ministry and ask, "Are they operating out of alignment?"

Be careful not to confuse cultural alignment with organizational agreement. Deceptively healthy churches often relish a false peace and harmony. We all want unity among the board, staff, and influencers. But the goal of total agreement has hurt churches and organizations in countless ways.

The goal in recalibrating your church is cultural alignment, not organizational agreement. Agreement is not only a warped perspective; it is an impossible goal. I have discovered that if everyone appears to agree, then either backbiting is taking place in the dark corners of the church, or everyone is so passive that they have not fully bought into the church's mission and vision. Therefore, the goal of recalibrating your church is cultural alignment, not organizational agreement.

Aligning the ministries and practices of your church will cause you the most pain you will ever experience as a leader. A cultural recalibration demands that you align your church, beginning with three alignment points.

1. Clarify your mission, ministry model, and core values

You may feel very frustrated right now. You might be saying, "I already *have* a mission statement!" or "I *have* core values!" or "I have a ministry model! We have all of those things, and yet *we're still in trouble!*" While your church won't necessarily move forward once these things are in place, without them, your church cannot reach its full Kingdom impact.

Here's the problem. A false notion in organizational theory claims if I have the right mission statement, the right core values, and the right ministry model and team, then my church will automatically grow and reach people for Christ. But think about that claim for a moment. If it were that easy, then would 80 percent of our churches be plateaued or in decline?

Mission statements, core values, and ministry models are essential, but if they do not align with the overall vision of the church, then they're not good for much beyond nice little quotes on a wall. These things have to be aligned with everything in your church.

Mission statement. Leaders need a clear and concise mission statement. Many churches have a mission statement that is really just a theological essay about church life. Such documents never help much, if at all. Does your mission statement align with your actual ministry practice? Does it come easily out of your mouth? When you pray or preach, do you find yourself habitually speaking about your mission statement, or do you have to force it? Is the mission statement personal, or just some catchy philosophical statement? Does it merely make you feel better about your church without prompting any change? Did the statement come passionately from your heart, or did it get hastily thrown together in a staff meeting? Does it cause you to dream bigger, think deeper, and move more quickly? All of these outcomes follow a well-crafted, passion-centered mission statement.

Core values. Core values guide an organization. At the end of the day, values motivate every action in your congregation. Your core values (and even values that you haven't identified as core) are essential. Ponder your core values. Do you live them out? Do they naturally come out during conversations? Do you like how they are worded? Do you even know them? Are they aligned with your real beliefs and behaviors? Do your core values align with the mission and ministry model?

Ministry model. While your ministry model is essential, it's a lot easier to create such a model than to actually use it. A lot of leaders have something they refer to as a ministry model. They've identified the five purposes of the church or the three keywords that define their church and have written them down somewhere. But the question is, do these *mean* anything? Or is this just a quick way to throw everything into a few buckets and call it a "ministry model"? Do you really use this model, across the board, for every age department?

2. Define mission-critical ministries and initiatives

When leading an established church, you have to define what is mission critical and what changes you can put on the back burner. We've already looked at this in detail in chapter 6.

If you create a mission statement, develop a ministry model and, identify some core values—but you fail to clearly link these to mission-critical ministries and initiatives—then you will *never* recalibrate your church. Talk alone accomplishes nothing.

3. Realign your resources

If you don't redirect your resources to your mission, values, ministry model and mission-critical ministries, then frankly, you are wasting your time—and probably injuring your church.

As mentioned already, New Life early on defined mission-critical ministries as weekend gatherings, kids' ministry, and groups. We decided to focus our energy and resources on removing anything that negatively impacted or drained energy from those three areas. If some activity or program did negatively impact one of those three things, then we would consider tweaking, changing, or even eliminating it.

I quickly realized this process was much easier to put on paper than to actually do. I learned I had to put my money where my mouth was . . . the truly difficult part of realigning our church's culture.

Five Resources: Put Your Money Where Your Mouth Is

You will never realign your church unless you realign your resources. This is where the rubber meets the road, where you hit the tarmac of alignment. This is where both leaders and the congregation put their money where their mouth is.

Every church, regardless of size, structure, or style, has a limited amount of resources. Are your limited resources arranged and positioned to strengthen your mission, values, and ministry model? Or does the way you use your resources actually compete with them?

Do you truly want to create a new cultural operating system at your church? If so, then consider these five resources that need to be carefully redirected for your congregation. These questions are not easy to answer! But if you dare to take an honest look at these five areas, and then take action to redirect your resources around your mission, ministry model, and a few mission-critical initiatives, then you will watch as a new, healthier COS takes root in your church.

1. Restructure your staff

Realigning your culture requires that you restructure your staff around your mission, values, ministry model, and mission-critical initiatives. And believe me, that can be very hard.

Whenever leaders talk about change, one of the elephants in the room is their current staff. They know it, but they don't want to say it. Deep down, they understand that the current staff is out of alignment.

One common example is children's ministry. We say, "We value children's ministry," but then we frequently fail to resource it with people. It is inconsistent for a church to say, "Our children's ministry is mission critical," but then hire every other staff member before children's ministry staff.

Are you willing to make tough decisions about staffing, based on mission-critical initiatives and ministries? Show me your staffing structure, and I will show you what is *really* mission critical in your church.

When I started leading New Life, we had two full-time youth pastors and two full-time choir/worship/orchestra directors, but very limited staffing for the children's ministry. Do you see the unintended choice we had made? By our actions, we said the music and youth ministries were more mission critical to our church than the children's ministry.

We also lacked sufficient staffing to facilitate Sunday's worship and creative elements, or give adequate leadership and oversight to our ministry for groups. So we made some changes. Restructuring the staff caused me more pain than any other decision I made at New Life.

2. Redirect your volunteers and leaders

Most churches think they have a volunteer problem. They don't. They have an alignment problem. Our people often fail to volunteer, not because they're lazy, but because the church is misaligned.

> **Our people often fail to volunteer, not because they're lazy, but because the church is misaligned.**

When pastors and leaders come to check out New Life, they often express some surprise at seeing the large number of parking lot attendants, greeters, and ushers. If they spend any time in our children's ministry, they find good adults leading and serving our kids. While we always need more volunteers, why do we have so many people serving in these key areas at our weekend gatherings, while other churches struggle? It's simple. Nothing else competes for their time.

Remember, we don't have an adult Sunday school program that keeps our best adults sitting and learning in a classroom. We don't have a full choir and orchestra that take up the time of a large number of potential volunteers. Our people serve in areas that we have identified as mission critical.

Think about the misalignment in most churches. We tell our people, "We want you to attend church, invite your friends, go to an adult Sunday school class, be in choir, and sign up to be an usher, greeter, or parking lot attendant—and by the way, be sure to sit together as a family in church." That's misalignment on all levels! People can't follow all these instructions in a balanced or healthy fashion.

3. Reorganize your finances

The easiest way to spot misalignment is to closely examine your finances. Your budget will reveal the reality of your ministry model and your mission-critical ministries. Money doesn't lie. As I've said, show me how you spend your church dollars, and I will show you your mission, values, and ministry model.

At New Life, we had to wrestle with a main staple of our identity: musical productions. Our church has had a rich history of the Singing Christmas Tree and many other outstanding productions. But as we redefined our mission model and identified our mission-critical changes, we had to ask ourselves some very probing and piercing questions. How could we reconcile the fact that the money we spent on productions exceeded what we gave to fund kids' ministry, group ministry, and even creating a warm and contagious environment on Sunday morning? When we examined all of our musical productions in light of our core ministries and priorities, the answer was clear.

4. Repurpose your facilities

I can walk into any church and almost immediately identify its ministry model. It's right before my eyes. Your ministry model determines how you use your facilities. Just look around! Your facilities say everything about your mission and ministry model.

You may be arguing with me right now. "That's easy for you to say," you object, "when you have that big building." I don't deny there's some truth to that claim. But my experience tells me that the size of your building doesn't matter much. I want to know what your facility usage says about your ministry model and focus.

When we built our new facility, I can't tell you how many specific items people wanted to include in the design. But since we had decided to build for Sundays, kids, and groups, here are the things we decided not to build, based upon our mission critical ministries:

- Full commercial kitchen
- Room for choir and orchestra
- Prayer tower
- More offices for pastors
- Adult Sunday school rooms
- Youth facilities
- Book store / resource center
- Athletic club / workout facility
- Wedding chapel

I kept reminding everyone, "We are building a facility to strengthen our Sunday gatherings, children's ministry, and life groups. That's all." We decided to build only for the mission-critical ministries we had identified and not for every ministry. That meant that everything listed above got left out of our building plans. And even with life groups, we decided that since the vast majority would meet offsite, we didn't want to create space for them in the building.

5. Restructure your calendar and communication bandwidth

I discuss these together because they're intrinsically linked. When I work with churches, I often bring up the problem of too many announcements. An overabundance of announcements is a core symptom that your church is misaligned. You have too many things going on. Your announcements yell every Sunday, "You are misaligned!"

How can you make sure the service doesn't get cluttered with announcements? You start with your calendar and then create a communication plan. Can you get your announcements down to ninety seconds? That's about the time of a long commercial break on television. If you are in alignment and highlighting only the mission-critical things, you can do this!

Time for Spring Cleaning

It is not a matter of if your church needs a spring cleaning, but when it will need one. You need a season when you find a couple of large plastic bags and a few dumpsters. Throw some stuff away! While I'm using metaphoric language here, it may quite literally be true for you. Slide projectors and felt-board characters, I'm looking at you!

Compulsive hoarding will throw your church out of alignment. So schedule those tough conversations with staff members whom you love. Look hard at every ministry and program and ask, "Is this in alignment?"

You can ignore alignment, but you can't avoid it.

As a leader, you are the one responsible to bring all of your volunteers, ministries, and programs into alignment with the church's values and mission. It's true that some programs will not survive the scrutiny. Some members won't join you in the transition.

But your mission is worth every bit of the pain. And if it's not, then you need a new mission.

Coaching Assignments

1. Take some time to frankly examine (or create) your mission, ministry model, core values, and mission-critical ministries. Ask yourself:

   • Does this resonate with us deeply?

   • Have we organized our ministries around these?

   • Are they incorporated into everyday church life?"

2. In what areas and practical ways is your church aligned? In what areas and practical ways are you misaligned?

3. Put your money where you mouth is.

   • How do you need to realign your resources?

   • How may you need to restructure your staff?

   • What steps can you make to redirect your best leaders and volunteers?

   • How can you begin the process of reorganizing your finances?

   • Where can you begin to repurpose your facilities?

   • What is your first step to restructure your calendar and communication?

8

PRACTICE #4
DEVELOP A CULTURAL LEXICON:
Language Creates Culture

One night many years ago, I was walking down the streets of Kirkland, Washington, discussing with some trusted friends my frustration with the culture of New Life. "How does one go about leading effective change?" I wondered aloud.

One of my friends looked at me and replied, "Language creates culture." He probably saw the puzzled expression on my face and added, "Think about it. Every society, business, and family culture is created around language. When you walk into Disneyland, an Apple Store, or Starbucks, you are introduced to an entirely new language. Customers are called guests, tech support staff are called geniuses, and a large-sized drink is called a 'Venti.'"

My friend's brief lesson on language stopped me right in the middle of the street. It became a true "Eureka!" moment in my life.

I quickly thought about Starbucks. I thought about the secret language of ordering a cup of coffee. Iced or hot? Size? Caf or Decaf? Milk? Syrup? Shots? Did you know that Starbucks estimates that its customers can choose from about 87,000 possible permutations of a drink?

The other day, my wife and I drove up to a Starbucks window to order: "A tall iced Americano with an extra shot, two pumps sugar-free vanilla, ounce of heavy cream, and a shake of cinnamon." Honestly, I live in Seattle, and I still don't get it. I asked myself, why would anyone say all these words for a cup of coffee? And then pay four dollars for it?

The answer is that people are not buying coffee; they are buying culture. How does Starbucks create this kind of appealing culture? It understands language and how to infuse the culture it wants to create in everyone who walks into one of its 21,366 stores around the world. And how does it manage this extraordinary feat? Starbucks understands that *language creates culture.*

That one statement changed my life. It has become a core transferable principle for recalibrating any congregation or organization.

What Kind of Culture Are You Creating?

Realigning a culture depends in large part on the words leaders choose and how they speak them to their congregation, staff, and board. Words have the power to shape not only lives, but also an organization's culture.

We've all heard the adage, "Sticks and stones may break my bones, but words will never hurt me." We often try to downplay the power of words and elevate the power of action. But words unquestionably are a powerful and effective means for transforming the cultural DNA of your church and aligning the church. Far more than you may think, the very language you use infuses cultural DNA into your congregation.

In his exceptional and well-researched work, *Organizational Culture and Leadership,* Edgar H. Schein shows how leaders use language to create and reinforce new culture: "Culture supplies us our language, and language provides meaning in our day-to-day life."[52] Any leader who wants to change a church's culture must first change the congregation's language.

Language is the essence of culture—how you say something, what you say, when you say it, the tone and inflection of your voice, everything. It all creates the culture of your church. Every word you speak in staff meetings, at board meetings, from the pulpit, when you feel frustrated, when you feel happy, when you're not even thinking about it—all of it helps to define the culture of your organization.

Chand uses strong language to communicate how words mold organizations: "Words have the power to shape lives and organizations. Too often, however, leaders aren't aware of their vocabulary as they speak, and they don't realize how people are affected by their words. Even casually spoken statements can have profound effects. The words we use, and the way we use them, define organizational culture."[53]

Your language, your tone, the meaning behind the words you use, what you laugh at, what makes you emotional— all of these things help to define your organizational culture. Language shapes myriad things, including the attitudes in your organization, the behaviors of your people, and the values that guide and define your future.

> The answer is that people are not buying coffee; they are buying culture.

Kouzes and Posner have concluded that exemplary leaders pay close attention to their language and choose their words with great care: "The words people choose to use are metaphors for concepts that define attitudes, behaviors, structures, and systems. Your words can have a powerful effect on how your constituents see their world, and you should choose them intentionally and carefully.[54]

This may shock you, but the cultural hurdles that cause the greatest problems are in fact created (or at least reinforced) by the language used in your church. Consider the following cultural problems that many churches commonly face.

Think about how your language might be creating a culture characterized by the following:

Lack of volunteers. I consistently hear leaders say, "No one volunteers at my church," or "We never have enough nursery workers." Your church hears you and believes you! As a result, no one volunteers.

When I say "no one," you obviously get some overly guilty people, but they volunteer because of pressure rather than culture. You have created or reinforced this culture without even knowing it, through your use of language. Change your language to say things like, "The heroes of this church are the many people who serve our kids. Every one of them is what makes our church a great community."

Silos. Like the tall, vertical storage cylinders used to store grain on most farms, the Silo Effect reflects a mindset of those who care only about their own goals, isolated by choice from (and not communicating with) others who are not a part of their team. Leaders create this type of dysfunctional culture with the very words they use.

Listen to the language used by your pastoral staff, core leaders, and volunteers. At New Life, we have forbidden the use of "they," a fundamentally dysfunctional word. If you hear people say things like, "*They* (referring to another ministry) always leave everything a mess," or in referring to the board, "*They* made this decision," then you know you have a cultural language problem. The language reveals an adversarial, "us vs. them" culture.

When your people talk about children's ministry, youth ministry, or any ministry, train them to use the language of "we," as in, "*We* reach kids," or "*We* serve youth," or "*We* love the community." Word choice is not trivial, nor is it silly. It's how language creates culture.

Negative attitudes toward unchurched people. Many churches speak of the unchurched in terms that make it difficult for unchurched people to visit. Churches often communicate their disdain for "the world" or spend entire sermons on political or cultural issues, rather than on Jesus and the cross. They speak of outsiders as enemies to be fought instead of friends to be redeemed. Chand laments that the message we send to outsiders is often "exclusive—and even offensive—to people in the community we are trying to reach with the message of Christ."[55]

At New Life, I wanted to create a church that unchurched people love to attend. I wanted to build a church where followers of Jesus would get excited about inviting and bringing people who are far from God. That required a culture shift.

I remember the first time I said, in the middle of my message, "If you are not a Christian, it's great to have you here. You may struggle with the some of the concepts of Scripture—no problem. I struggle with many of the things the Bible says, too." Talk about infusing new cultural DNA into the bloodstream of the church! I made the decision to be as open and vulnerable to our guests as I wanted them to be with us. I remember the looks I got from some members of my congregation. At first, I could tell they were thinking, *This is strange.* But over time, their faces told me a different story: *This is normal.* By changing our language, our people became excited about inviting people to New Life.

Anti-number attitudes. This may feel too pointed, but many church leaders create a culture that opposes numerical growth. As we saw in chapter 2, there are some very solid reasons why numbers may or may not be growing at your church. Too often, though, growth is flat or even retrograde because the leadership has created a dys-functional culture *against* numerical growth.

You might feel very surprised at how easy it is to create language that prevents your church from growing. I have heard leaders say things like this:

"One of the great things about this church is we all know each other."

"We are not like the big church down the street. We have more depth than them."

"God is not about numbers."

Almost every time I've heard a leader say something like this, it's code for, "We're not growing, and this language helps us to feel better about ourselves." Very often, it's a way for dispassionate leaders to justify the failings of their church. They use language to frame their lack of growth as an advantage, trying to disguise the fact that vision, energy, and focus on the unchurched have all dissipated some time ago.

Creating a Cultural Lexicon

Most of us are familiar with J.R.R. Tolkien's epic saga *The Lord of Rings*. Within his complex and highly detailed fantasy world live dozens of creatures, humans, elves, trolls, and other memorable creations. Many people do not know, however, that in order to fully develop the imaginative realm of Middle-earth, Tolkien, a well-respected phi-lologist, developed intricate and exhaustive languages for each of his imaginary species. From elves to dwarves to orcs, Tolkien knew that creating a language was the beginning of creating a culture.

> As you listen to the language used by your church, remember that you are listening to the heart of your church.

As the leader, you must develop an intricate and exhaustive lexicon for how you approach church, your culture, and your ministries. Infusing new cultural DNA into your church will require you to learn an entirely new language, and then figure out how to infuse this language into the heart of your church. Consider three key steps to creating a new cultural lexicon at your church:

1. Listen to the current language of your church

Just by listening to the language I hear in your church, I can tell you practically everything about your church or organization. Does that sound like a simplistic statement? In some ways, I suppose it is; yet, your church *does* have a cultural language that communicates its beliefs, behaviors, and values.

Allow me to give you what may be the strangest coaching assignment in this book. For one week, listen carefully to the language of your church. Pay close attention. What does the language communicate? What kind of culture is it helping to create? Does your current language resonate with the kind of church you want to become? Listen to some very specific things during this week:

Pay painstakingly close attention to the words spoken and the tone used in your Sunday service: Is your language full of church talk and Christianese? How would a person outside of the faith feel if they heard you talk? Is this a culture that you would invite someone to come and experience with you?

Take some time to listen to one of your messages: What kind of culture are you creating? Do you like your own preaching?

Listen to your language in your board meetings: Does the language create synergy with the church? Does the language reflect trust? Do you have a board that resonates with the mission, or does the language used there reveal a desire merely to protect the status quo?

Carefully reflect on the language during staff meetings: What kind of culture are you creating? Primarily positive or negative? Welcoming or cold? Engaging or adversarial?

What values do you see reinforced? What do your people say the most? What specific words get used most frequently?

Jesus told us that the mouth speaks whatever fills the heart (Luke 6:45). As you listen to the language used by your church, remember that you are listening to the heart of your church. How would you describe that heart, based on what you hear? What is going on inside? What fills your church? Be brutally honest here! Listening to the language of your church helps you to understand the reality of your current culture and the heart of your church. It allows you to get a grip on the current cultural reality.

2. Craft a new cultural lexicon

Schein suggests that organizations must come together to "establish a system of communication and a language that permits setting goals and interpreting and managing what is going on."[56] Organizations of every type must create a common language and universal conceptual categories: "If members cannot communicate with and understand each other, a group is impossible by definition."[57]

Where do you begin? How can you create a cultural lexicon for your own congregation?

Involve your staff, board and even a group of influencers. Meet with these groups. Find a whiteboard to record some brainstorming ideas on possible new language you could use.

Turn your mission statement, ministry model, and core values into everyday language. Leaders often create a mission statement or core values, but never infuse them into the everyday language of their churches. The starting point for creating a common language is your mission statement, core values, and ministry model. This may seem like a "duh" statement, but those three elements should generate the lexicon of your language.

One litmus test for me on the mission and values of a church is this: Do I naturally use these words and phrases without having to announce that I am about to use them? When I am praying, do I pray these words? If your mission doesn't flow out of your mouth in a natural and authentic way, it is not resonating with you deeply. So rethink it. Rewrite it. And then speak it frequently and with passion.

Develop key words and phrases. Grab a journal or open up a Word document and begin to jot down words. Think in terms of creating a small dictionary. What words do you want to start using? How would you define them simply?

Develop potent metaphors, stories, and narratives. Creating a culture lexicon requires a leader to think through the metaphors, narratives, and stories that create the cultural norms in a church. Leaders have to make sure they infuse the right metaphors into the bloodstream of the church.

One of my doctoral classes, "Cultural Exegesis Reimagining Missional Ministry," was taught by noted author and church thinker Leonard Sweet. This class transformed and recalibrated my own personal leadership. Sweet talked about the power of metaphors, narratives, and stories. He claimed that the average church member takes in 3,500 sermons a day through media and outside interactions, almost all of them in the form of a metaphor or image.

> Healthy organizations update, tweak, and make continuous improvements to their language.

"When you dream," he asked, "do you dream in words?" The answer is obvious. We dream in images, stories, metaphors, and narrative. Sweet created a new word (what scholars call a "neologism"), combining "narratives" with "metaphor" to create the new term, "narraphors."

A narraphor I use often at New Life is the story told in chapter 5 about the "Young Turks" of 1979, when Darrell Jones provided $20 as earnest money for our current property. People love the powerful story of how a one board member can make a huge difference. The metaphor of $20 is practical and yet moving at the same time; a metaphor for how little sacrifices can make a big difference. It's an incredible narraphor telling how God can use normal, everyday people to make a significant Kingdom impact!

Recalibrate your language often. Part of a continually recalibrating culture is regularly rethinking and recreating language. Often, we will be talking in the middle of a staff meeting and someone will use a memorable word or phrase. I will remind myself to add this to our language sheet.

Healthy organizations update, tweak, and make continuous improvements to their language. You might be reading a book, watching a movie, or talking to a friend, when someone will use a phrase or a word you love. Add this to your lexicon and common language sheet.

New Life has created a "Cultural Language Sheet." This document spells out all of our preferred language in words, phrases, and metaphors. If you would like a copy of the New Life Language Sheet, you can visit my website at www.recalibrategroup.com/resources.

3. Guard your new lexicon

Leaders have to infuse a new cultural language and then guard it with bulldog tenacity. Everyone has a cultural lens through which they see church and form opinions on how church should be done. Every new person and every new staff member you bring on the team already has a church culture from somewhere else that they bring to the table.

It is easy to assume that new people will automatically pick up on your new language, but this doesn't always happen. You must create environments where you teach people the language of your church. It's almost like taking every new staff member or person to "language school."

Schein points out one of the greatest mistakes leaders make when integrating new members: "One of the cultural traps that new organizations face is the failure to note that new members come from very different subcultures and need to establish a common meaning system within the common language."[58] Practically speaking, if someone comes into your church from another church (perhaps an opposite model or style), they may struggle to adopt the language and culture of your church. If they rise in leadership or influence, this could create dysfunction. It is important to create environments where your lexicon and language can be reinforced, both continually and naturally.

This becomes evident at New Life in an environment we call New Life 101, our "language school" for people new to our church. It provides an opportunity for them to meet the pastors, hear the heart and soul of our church, and learn how to connect. It regularly startles me to see how new people (especially if they come from other churches) bring in their own cultural language. This is why you have to carefully, intentionally, and regularly teach, speak, and guard your language.

This becomes particularly true with new staff members. Bringing on new staff is by far the most complicated challenge in regard to safeguarding the cultural language of your church. Every new staff member brings to the table some type of church and leadership culture. Hybels says he looks for three things in new staff members: character, chemistry, and competency.[59] I have added a fourth one: culture. Culture is the thing that can most hurt a staff relationship and damage the language of the church. It takes one to two years just to teach new staff members the cultural language of New Life.

Theological Language and One Pastor's Struggle

During one coaching session with a pastor, I got the sense he wanted to ask a question, but didn't know if he should. Finally he got up the nerve: "How do I deal with people in my church who are 'spiritually weird'?" he asked. Honestly, this is a very common question I get when I work with pastors of established churches.

I smiled, because I knew *exactly* who he was talking about: the sincere people who want to demonstrate their particular gifts of the Spirit during a public service in a way that makes the pastor cringe. The subject of the Holy Spirit often causes great debate and confusion in the Christian world. In many ways, I think the problem is rooted in bad language.

I told him, "You have a language problem, not a theological problem. Listen to yourself talk. You keep on speaking about the Holy Spirit as an 'it' instead of as a Person. You need to change your language. Recalibrate for your people the biblical language Scripture uses to talk about the Holy Spirit. Create a new cultural lexicon for how you talk about the Holy Spirit, and then guard it with bulldog tenacity."

Then I said, "Don't be defensive when you do this, and don't try to prove a point. Just develop a sound theological lexicon about the Holy Spirit. Use language that resonates deeply with you and doesn't make you cringe."

A light almost instantly seemed to turn on in his head. "My entire denomination needs to rethink the language we use to help people understand the work of the Holy Spirit in the life of a believer," he said.

Yes, your language *does* matter. Don't forget: language creates culture!

Coaching Assignments

1. Spend one week listening to the language of your church. What does your language tell you about your culture? What cultural norms might you be unintentionally creating?

2. Begin to craft a new cultural lexicon. Write down words, phrases, metaphors, narratives, and stories that capture the kind of language you believe God wants to infuse into your church.

3. How can you guard the cultural language of your church? In what specific environments can new people catch the cultural language of your church?

9

PRACTICE #5
CELEBRATE SHORT-TERM WINS:
Tangible Examples of the New Cultural Norm

As I wrote this book, one of my executive pastors decided to surprise me and "made" me go to a Seattle Seahawks game, my first time at Seattle's Century Link Field. I have to admit, I felt very excited.

The 12th Man fan base in Seattle is beyond fanatical and well known for the noise it generates. At one point, it held the record for the loudest stadium crowd in the world, registering 137.5 decibels. To put that in perspective, a jet engine at 100 feet generates 140 decibels. Opponents playing in Seattle average 2.36 false starts per game, a statistic attributed to the rabid fan base of Seattle's 12th Man.

Experiencing the noise amazed me. It really was beyond belief! Seahawks fans celebrated every time the ball moved forward. One yard, three yards, first down, it didn't matter. From the moment the Seahawks came out on the field, the 12s made noise. From one-yard gains to touchdowns, the 12s went crazy. It was fun to see them distract the opposing team.

At the end, everyone thought the Hawks had lost the game when Detroit's Calvin Johnson stretched out at the goal line to try to score

. . . but he fumbled. Seattle linebacker K.J. Wright slapped the ball out of bounds to save the game. The rules say you can't do that, but the refs missed the call, and Seattle won, 13-10.

Talk about noise!

Can you imagine if the 12s celebrated only when the Seahawks scored a touchdown? What if they sat politely after each first down, every interception, every returned kick? What if they mimicked a library, quiet between each play? The games would bore everyone, including the players. The entire ethos of Seattle football is built around the fact that Seahawks fans celebrate every time the team moves the ball downfield. The 12s make noise at every level, every move in the right direction, every win.

Church leaders could take a few pointers from the 12s. One key way to infuse new cultural DNA into the bloodstream of your church—and build the momentum and congregational morale you need—is to "celebrate short-terms wins."

The Practice That Turned the Tide

You've already heard that my first three years of pastoring were hell on earth. I found myself in the middle of the most stretching and discouraging leadership period of my life. It felt as though every day I woke up to a new leadership nightmare. People were complaining loudly and leaving the church. Moreover, the pastoral staff felt upset because of my decisions. Although some good things were happening at New Life, I felt like I was drowning in hate mail and sinking in a quagmire of gossip and rumors.

Perhaps the most common question leaders have asked me is this: "How did you keep New Life on track while leading the church into significant change?"

That's easy. I celebrated short-term wins! Without exaggeration, I can say that the only human reason I made it through the first three years at New Life is that I celebrated the wins and didn't indulge the losses. I celebrated every time New Life moved the ball forward one yard, three yards, and whenever we got a first down. I celebrated every *small* win.

I celebrated during my messages, at board meetings, opening up staff meetings, talking to people in the lobby, and talking to influencers. I started to celebrate every new person, every new baptism, every special offering, and every positive comment I overheard in the community. With every win, I celebrated. Celebrating short-term wins helped us to turn the tide from a negative, everyone's-leaving-the-church vibe, to a positive, God-is-doing-something-special-at-New Life vibe.

> **Without exaggeration, I can say that the only human reason I made it through the first three years at New Life is that I celebrated the wins and didn't indulge the losses.**

University of Michigan professor Karl Weick describes a short-term win as "a concrete, complete, implemented outcome of moderate importance."[60] Here's my own definition of a short-term win: "A tangible example of the new cultural norm." Short-term wins are specific and concrete examples of the new culture that the leader is intentionally infusing into the DNA of the church. Short-term wins help people feel and taste the new norm before the new norm becomes normal.

The Most Frustrating Time of Change

In his book *Organization Development: The Process of Leading Organizational Change*, Donald Anderson describes a time when "neither the old nor the new ways work properly"—the most frustrating time in a change initiative. He refers to this season as the "neutral zone" and explains in detail the emotional roller coaster people are riding during this time.

People may feel:

> Frustrated and confused to recognize that a change is taking place, without the comfort of established routines and practices

> Bombarded and overwhelmed by new information, unsure how to evaluate or interpret it all

> Uncomfortable, since it feels risky to try new things without the knowledge of what may happen next

> Unnerved, as if the transition is taking forever without a clear sense of when the confusion will end.[61]

In the neutral zone, such feelings are all normal and to be expected. A time will come when the old no longer works and the new has yet to embed fully in the culture. In that time, a leader must celebrate every win, no matter how insignificant it may seem. Celebrating short-term wins will help people deal with their frustrations, confusions, and uncomfortable tensions during a recalibration.

Anyone who has done a home remodel project understands the frustrating neutral zone phase. One of the most frustrating times during the renovation occurs right in the middle, that period when the old parts of the house have been demolished and no longer function, but the new is not working either (and often not even within eyesight of working).

Dust is everywhere. Nothing is complete. Walls gape open. It seems as though the project will never end.

I have done many remodeling projects on my historic 1896 home and have learned that you have to celebrate every small win along the way. I have to keep my wife up-to-date on the contractor's progress—not hard at the beginning, when progress is easy to see. But when the time comes for the electrical and plumbing and everything else that goes behind the walls, the project can become very long and mind numbing.

The most frustrating time during a change initiative, like a home remodel, is when the old no longer works and the new has not yet caught on. During the neutral zone of any change, leaders have to learn how to celebrate short-term wins.

Consider these three tangible reasons to celebrate every short-term win.

1. It builds morale

Perhaps one of the most difficult challenges facing a leader is building morale during the neutral zone. Your people tend to feel as though innovation and cultural change won't work. People start complaining, feeling frustrated because the old is gone and the new isn't working, and are tempted to give up and just throw in the towel.

Leaders must be concerned about the mission of the church and the morale of the church, both at the same time. Far too often, you hear language like, "We are all about the mission, regardless of the cost." While this is true at one level, your slumping morale will hurt the mission in the long run.

In the neutral zone, leaders must celebrate the short-term wins that prove the changes are working and that progress toward a new and effective church is taking place. Leaders focused entirely on outcomes forget that they must bring others along on the journey with them. Staff and volunteers don't always have the advantage of seeing the big picture and can get focused exclusively on their little silos and how the changes affect them. They get frequent complaints and mixed messages. They often hear the grumbles and rumors that you will never hear and so absorb most of the discontentment. This can influence their personal thoughts and feelings, creating a more volatile situation.

Celebrating short-term wins builds morale by letting people know their efforts are paying off and the changes are actually working. In Leading Change, Kotter discusses eight stages for leading organizational transformation and calls the sixth stage "Generating Short-Term Wins." He admits that since major changes take time, people "want and need convincing evidence that all their efforts are paying off. They want to see clear data indicating that the changes are working."[62]

People need to see progress, or else the plunging morale of your people will stifle the life out of your church. Your coworkers will not stay the course unless you find ways to give them hope. We all need clear data to build morale that the changes are working.

2. It reinforces culture

A short-term win is a tangible example of the new cultural norm. Every time you celebrate a short-term win, therefore, you reinforce the new culture you want in your church.

A bit of warning here: leaders must be very careful what they celebrate. Since what you celebrate reinforces both good and dysfunctional culture, what you celebrate should align with your mission, core values, ministry model, mission-critical changes, and the culture you want to craft within your church.

It's easy for churches to celebrate deceptively healthy practices, such as a crammed church calendar or overly busy people. Make sure you celebrate only the new aspects of your DNA and not the former, negative ones. Take care that you don't unintentionally reinforce dysfunctional behavior by celebrating old habits and outdated traditions.

At New Life, I wanted to create a culture that would effectively reach young families. I therefore decided to celebrate every win connected to this cultural change. I remember the first time I did this. A young couple told me how much their kids loved the church and how much they also enjoyed it. I stood up the next Sunday and said, "The other day I was at Starbucks, and a couple approached me to let me know how much they loved New Life. They loved the parking lot attendants, the kids' workers, and the warmth of the people."

At first, it felt as though I were speaking a foreign language, but eventually, our people started catching it. Mind you, at this time I heard the comment only once or twice. But since I longed for New Life to become this, I intentionally reinforced the culture of reaching young families, no matter how insignificant the incident.

3. It cultivates momentum

When you celebrate a short-term win, you cultivate momentum. As we've seen, God creates momentum, and leaders either cultivate or stifle that momentum, just as a surfer can catch a wave or get crushed by it. Leaders must know how to catch and cultivate the momentum that God sends. Celebrating short-term wins gives us a means to harness and cultivate the momentum God is sending to us.

Or think of it as gaining traction. Traction refers to a footing or a grip. Celebrating short-term wins helps leaders gain a footing or grip on the new culture they want to build. Leaders move the mission forward inch by inch and yard by yard. Short-term wins help people move forward incrementally in the new direction and give them confidence that the vision anchored in the leader's heart is not merely talk.

In his book *Change Your Church or Die*, Josh Hunt describes the need for short-term wins: "Without short-term wins the change process will never gain traction. Fairly early on we need to find some early successes, no matter how small, and put a spotlight on them."[63]

In the history of World War II, no battle holds more significance than D-Day, the invasion of Normandy. In order for the Allies to successfully invade Nazi-occupied Europe, they needed to establish a beachhead, an area on the coast of France where combined forces could launch the larger attack into Axis territory. Supreme Allied Commander Dwight Eisenhower knew that if he could establish a footing in northern France, he could go all the way into Germany. And that's exactly what he did.

Short-term wins provide those footings, the beachheads that allow leaders to successfully build an initiative and cultivate momentum for transformational change.

Share Stories

Appropriate stories reinforce culture, build morale, and cultivate momentum with a power unmatched by anything else. If you want to celebrate short-term wins, know that stories are better than stats. Celebrate people, not just projects and outcomes.

I agree with the old saying, "A picture is worth a thousand words." Stories paint a vibrant picture in the minds of your people. A story that helps the recalibration process is a tangible example of the new cultural norm. The best way to infuse cultural DNA into your church is through a narraphor, a compelling narrative that strengthens a metaphor. While alliterated points and pithy sayings may catch a few ears, nothing will communicate your church's mission better than a good story. Stories impact the heart and provide concrete examples of your mission in action, so learn to weave the small wins into the framework of a story of a changed life.

Kouzes and Posner explain why leaders should use stories to shape culture and define the core of the organization: "Stories are another powerful tool for teaching people about what's important and what's not, what works and what doesn't, what is and what could be. Through stories, leaders pass on lessons about shared values and get others to work together."[64]

While nothing is wrong with providing stats, too often leaders drift toward celebrating them, especially those around attendance, finances, numbers of conversions, baptisms, or attendance at special events or group meetings. No doubt the church can celebrate these milestones; stats can be helpful and even encouraging to the people in an organization. But make no mistake, stories always move the heart and soul of your people and more quickly create a new organizational culture. Why is this so?

I can think of several reasons;

- Stories focus on people, and people move the hearts of other people.
- Stories remove any question of the leader's motive for change.
- Stories relate to people far better than stats.
- Stories connect the dots to help people understand why you are doing what you're doing.

Are small groups a priority for you? If so, find a story of someone who has been remarkably impacted by a small group and share that story with your church.

Very early on, I created a place in the bulletin called "Stories of Changed Lives." Every week, I inserted a quote from someone who reported being positively impacted by the changes at New Life. I shouted out their stories. I also incorporated their stories into my messages. This, too, provided people with hope. They started thinking, *These changes are actually working.* People have to believe recalibration is not mere talk, but that it works in the lives of real people.

Start Today!

Celebrating short-term wins is the easiest and most enjoyable leadership practice in this book. This single transferable practice produces maximum results with minimal effort and it doesn't cost you a dime. Most leaders can begin to use it today. Even the most cynical and critical people will respond.

Although this one practice can build momentum and boost morale more effectively than any other during the recalibration process, somehow it is one of the most overlooked, underused, and disregarded tools of a leader. An astonishing number of leaders don't celebrate short-term wins. Somehow, many leaders think you celebrate only when you score the big touchdown. They've never understood that the reason you don't score a big touchdown is because you haven't celebrated the small wins along the way.

Pastors often ask me, "Where and how do I celebrate short-term wins?" I think some of the best places to celebrate short-term wins are within the "intentional environments" of your church.

We have several such environments at New Life:

Whole staff meetings. Every Tuesday, New Life has a practice that has reinforced our culture and built amazing morale and momentum. We get the whole staff together in an environment we call "staff chapel" and celebrate wins from the weekend. This one environment infuses culture into the heart of New Life like very few other things we do with the team.

Sundays come every 165 hours. It is easy to push your staff Sunday to Sunday and not worry about the morale of your team members. And the truth is, good things happen every Sunday at your church—but most leaders don't stop and celebrate them. They let these wins go by without a single mention.

Take time to intentionally create an environment each week where your team, whether paid or volunteer, can celebrate the wins of the previous Sunday. A coffee time, a small group, or even a video chat meeting can provide the vehicle to communicate these wins.

Pre-service huddle. Every Sunday, we gather with all the musicians, production crew, ushers, greeters, parking lot attendants, guest services volunteers, and pastors for a short time to celebrate and cultivate culture. We do this from 8:45–8:55 am. Our service starts at 9:30. This gives our teams a time to huddle. During this time, we celebrate stories of changed lives.

Weekend gathering. The weekend gathering provides many great opportunities to celebrate short-term wins. During your message, share a story to illustrate a point or start off your message by describing something great God did this last week. Create a video where you show someone's story or celebrate a specific win at your church.

Board meetings. Leaders make a great mistake when they discuss only business with the board. At our board meetings, we celebrate wins together. I purposefully and intentionally create time to reflect on what God is doing in the church. Tell your own stories and share what is happening in your church. Celebrate those great things together!

Meet Derek

I first met my real estate agent, Derek Catherall, back in 2010. We got together at a local Starbucks. As I sat there, in walked this thirty-two-year-old, good-looking guy about whom I knew nothing.

One of the very first things Derek said to me was, "I am not a follower of Jesus. Before we start working together in real estate, I felt responsible to share this with you." (We had been emailing back and forth and somehow he discovered I was a pastor.)

"This is awesome," I replied, "no problem at all."

From that point on, Derek and I connected as friends. Over the next eighteen months, Derek helped me to navigate some tough real estate waters, due to the market crash of 2008. We talked, told stories, and developed a great friendship. Derek watched as I handled some complicated real estate transactions. He watched me deal with conflict, disappointment in the market, family issues, and saw something of my personal financial life. He had never before seen a follower of Jesus deal with real-life issues, and the experience softened his heart to the idea of Christianity.

At some point, Derek decided to come to church. He loved New Life. His family loved the church. Before I knew it, Derek was coming all the time. After eighteen months of building our friendship, I finally said to Derek, "Can we have the faith talk?"

He said yes.

Again we met at a local Starbucks. I asked him to tell me his story. Derek described a life filled with regrets and pain. He told me private details that made me feel deeply honored. "Derek," I eventually said, "can you tell me about your faith?"

He described his hesitations about God and the church. But after meeting a person who authentically lived out his faith, and after experiencing the vibrant culture at New Life for himself, something had changed in his life.

"Derek, may I share with you about Christ and His power to change your life?" I asked. I told him about the power of God's love and forgiveness and than asked another question: "Derek, would you like to surrender your life to Christ right now?"

To my surprise, he said, "Yes, right now." There we were, sitting in Starbucks, and I prayed a simple prayer of forgiveness and repentance with my friend. After we prayed, it was obvious that God had deeply touched Derek's life. As we walked out, Derek said to me, "We walked into Starbucks as friends. We are walking out as brothers."

I shared this story with New Life, and afterwards I personally baptized Derek in water. His story changed the heart and soul of New Life. *One* story. *One* celebration. *One* life.

I could have told our people, "Ninety-nine individuals gave their hearts to Christ last year." Certainly, the church could celebrate *that!* But when I told Derek's story, that moment of celebration changed everything.

Find your own Derek, and celebrate that story at your church. And then watch everything change.

Coaching Assignments

1. Write out a list of short-term wins. Then keep writing. Write down both the small ones and the big ones. Share these with your staff, board, and church.

2. For the next three Sundays, incorporate one short-term win in your message. Use it to illustrate a core point of your message.

3. Find a story of a changed life in your church. Interview this person. Perhaps even put this story on video. Share it with your staff, board, and church.

10

CAST CLEAR VISION:
The Catalyst for Meaningful and Lasting Change

I've asked many pastors, staff members, and church boards, "What makes you cringe at your church? If you were able to get over your fear of losing people, what would you stop doing immediately?"

Invariably, they can rattle off some kind of list, often a very long one. Most of us know what we don't like about our churches! We have a laundry list of items that make us cringe, items we desperately want to change.

It's easy to identify what we *don't* like. In fact, any punk can tell you everything he sees wrong with some church. Anyone can take a match and a can of gasoline and burn down a house. It doesn't take much skill to become an arsonist.

To rebuild a house, however, takes a good deal of skill. To rebuild a house takes careful planning, sufficient resources, and perhaps above all else, a set of blueprints that tells you exactly what the rebuilt house should look like.

God wants you as the leader of a church to become a skillful architect, not a reckless arsonist. It takes an effective leader to clarify exactly where the church should go and then cast this vision in a way that enables the people of the church to build well.

But how many of us have a clear vision of the future we *do* want? Anyone can tell you what is wrong with something, but it takes an effective leader to define what the new normal will be.

Vision: The Catalyst for Change

Realigning the culture of your church is not merely a campaign or some fancy "grow your church" crusade. It is about the leader infusing a new cultural DNA into the fabric of every nook and cranny of the church—and it is impossible to transform the cultural DNA of one's church or organization without a clear vision of the future.

The catalyst for meaningful and lasting change is vision. As we saw in chapter 1, a catalyst in science is "an element that speeds up the rate and power of a chemical reaction." The element that speeds up the rate of change in a church is clear vision.

> The job of the leader is to look at his or her church and help it see the exciting and ennobling possibilities of the future.

In his book *Deep & Wide*, Stanley describes his personal leadership conviction about leading a change initiative: "The catalyst for introducing and facilitating change in the local church is a God-honoring, mouthwatering, unambiguously clear vision."[65] A mouthwatering vision of the future creates an appetite for change. Many people may not like change, but they love vision.

Stanley believes that a shared vision is not only the key to facilitating change, but also to maintaining a culture of momentum after the actual change occurs: "Once initial changes have been made, vision is the key to maintaining organizational focus and momentum. Shared vision is critical to getting your church on the right track and keeping it there."[66]

You can have good theology, godly living, prayers full of faith, and even great preaching, but without a clear vision, the church will slowly and steadily drift of mission and eventually stagnate. Clear vision is what moves the church forward—and yet, no doubt the toughest and most complex part of realigning the culture of your church is developing laser-beam vision.

Kouzes and Posner write of the imperative role of the leader as it relates to the future: "Leaders envision the future by imagining exciting and ennobling possibilities."[67] The job of the leader is to look at his or her church and help it see the exciting and ennobling possibilities of the future. If a leader misses this part of recalibration, there will be no catalyst for lasting, meaningful change.

Kotter provides three practical reasons for providing clear vision during a change initiative:

Vision simplifies hundreds or thousands of more detailed decisions.

Vision motivates people to take action in the right direction, even if the initial steps are personally painful.

Vision helps coordinate the actions of different people, even many thousands of individuals, in a remarkably fast and efficient way.[68]

Vision sparks a chain reaction in a congregation. Once people see the future, it creates an urgency to move forward. When a leader paints a clear and compelling word picture of the preferred future, the people in the church will make enormous sacrifices and take far-reaching action to accomplish this vision.

What Is Vision?

A ton of literature exists offering multiple perspectives on the nature of vision.

Let's start with what vision is not:

- Vision is not a merely a statement.
- Vision is not an unrealistic hope.

- Vision is not purely a business concept.
- Vision is not the appropriation of someone else's innovation.
- Vision is not a list of things you dislike.

Oxford Dictionary defines vision as: "The ability to think about or plan the future with imagination or wisdom."[69] Vision is a word picture. Kotter provides a helpful definition of vision: "Vision refers to a picture of the future with some implicit or explicit commentary on why people should strive to create that future."[70] People must be able see the vision, or it is not a vision.

Kouzes and Posner offer this incredible insight on vision: "The word vision itself has at its root the verb 'to see.' Statements of vision, then, should not be statements at all. They should be pictures, word pictures. They're more image than words. For a vision to be shared, it needs to be seen in the mind's eye."[71] Anytime leaders help their church see something that doesn't yet exist, they are casting a clear and compelling vision.

I define vision like this: "Vision is a clear image or picture of a future outcome that allows leaders, volunteers, and team members to conceptualize, engage, and execute initiatives." You have to stand before your people and paint a compelling picture of the preferred future. This is your job. You have to make your people see and feel how the future could look.

Think of vision in terms of architectural plans or blueprints. Leaders need to be architects of the vision, according to Kouzes and Posner, not slaves to the details of pressing problems: "Much as an architect draws a blueprint or an engineer builds a model, you need to have a clear vision of what the results should look like before starting any project."[72] If your people can't see it or imagine it, either you have not done a good job casting vision, or what you have is not a vision at all.

The best visions I have ever developed often started on a napkin at Starbucks or a picture in my journal or notepad. Drawing out a picture or using words that describe that future—this is vision. Vision is a picture, an image, or something concrete that your people can see in their mind's eye.

The ABCs of Vision Casting

It is one thing to have a vision; it's an entirely different thing to stand before your people and cast this vision. One of the primary reasons that church Relaunch Initiatives fail is that leaders miss the vital practice of casting a clear and compelling vision.

Casting vision is the catalyst for a continuous culture of recalibration in your church. A leader may have a clear vision, but if he or she cannot effectively cast the vision, the church will most naturally settle into the status quo. To "cast" literally means "to throw (something) forcefully in a specified direction." Leaders need to throw vision forcefully and clearly in a specified direction so that the church moves forward.

The great thing is that pastors have a built-in platform to cast vision every weekend. Everyone is listening. Pastors need to stand before their churches with a dream deeply embedded in their own souls and effectively communicate it.

> A leader may have a clear vision, but if he or she cannot effectively cast the vision, the church will most naturally settle into the status quo.

When you cast a clear vision, you put the element into play that will change everything at your church. A leader who learns the practice of casting vision will unite the staff, the board, key influencers, and the whole church. Once people can clearly *see* the future, it gets their blood pumping, minds racing, and pocket books opening.

I love to watch *Shark Tank* on Friday nights. On this show, entrepreneurs stand before four self-made millionaires/billionaires (the "sharks") and persuade them to invest in their companies. The entrepreneurs have just a few moments to cast a clear vision. Depending on their ability to cast their vision in three minutes or less, the sharks will invest in or reject the idea.

All metaphors eventually break down, but in this shark metaphor, your congregants are the sharks. (It's possible that in your case, this feels quite literal.) Your people are constantly asking, "Should we invest in your vision?" Leaders have only a few moments to convince the church to buy into the vision. If you can't cast your vision in three to five minutes or less, people won't listen to you.

> Don't make the mistake of associating vision with unrealistic and impossible dreams.

Consider a useful rule of thumb from Kotter: "Whenever you cannot describe the vision driving a change initiative in five minutes or less and get a reaction that signifies both understanding and interest, you are in for trouble.[73] You have to be able to cast your vision to someone in less than five minutes and get a positive response.

How does a leader cast vision?

How does a leader paint a picture of the preferred future for the church?

How does a leader throw vision forcefully in the direction of the people?

While these are complicated questions, I have identified three filters to help leaders cast a vision that will move a congregation forward. I call these the ABCs of vision casting.

1. Attainable

Don't make the mistake of associating vision with unrealistic and impossible dreams. When leaders cast vision, the people have to feel, *This is stretching, but not impossible.* Some church leaders cast vision so far out of reach that they lose credibility with their congregations. You can't afford to look like a reckless leader living in a fairytale land.

Every time I cast vision, I ask myself a very difficult question: do the people believe this is attainable, or do they think I'm just shouting loudly and creating a bunch of hype? If people don't consider the vision attainable, they will say "good idea," but never truly buy into the vision.

This is one reason why, throughout this book, I have maintained that leaders must "date it." Without an activation date, the vision will never get traction. Anytime I cast vision, I use a precise date. Dates have a way of convincing people the leader is serious. Dates make the vision seem attainable. Once you announce a date, it brings the future into the present. If I start my vision casting saying, "In nine months, here is what God is going to do," people listen. The date itself makes it feel attainable.

2. Believable

When you cast vision, both the leader and the vision need to feel believable. People have to believe in both the person and in the vision, or they will not take you seriously.

For a vision to be believable, people to have trust and believe in the leader. Kouzes and Posner insist that "Credibility is the foundation of leadership. Constituents must be able, above all else, to believe in their leaders. For them to willingly follow someone else, they must believe that the leader's word can be trusted, that she is personally passionate and enthusiastic about the work, and that she has the knowledge and skill to lead."[74]

Three questions will help a leader discover if some proposed vision is believable:

Do you believe the vision? This may sound odd, but far too many leaders don't believe their own visions. They read some book that told them to cast vision, so they came up with one—but the vision does not burn deep down inside of them. They may speak the words, but deep down inside, they don't believe the vision themselves.

Can people see the vision in their mind's eye? After vision casting, ask yourself this question about your congregation. People can't "see" merely a bunch of words and a pile of data. Remember, people dream in pictures and images, not words and concepts.

Can people see themselves participating in this vision? A significant part of the "believable" factor is people seeing how they fit into the vision. You have to drive the vision down to reality. You have to give them pictures, stories, and examples that will prompt them to say, "Oh, I can be a part of this!"

3. Compelling

The dream has to be compelling, irresistible, and convincing. "Compelling" means to evoke interest, attention, or admiration in a powerfully irresistible way. Vision casting means a leader evokes interest, attention, or admiration in a vision in a powerfully irresistible way.

People do not have to feel so stunned by your glowing vision of the future that they give you a standing ovation. But it has to make a person say, "Wow!" It has to be something that seems so believable, so real, that it makes them pause and say to themselves, "Okay, we can do this." In the church world, they have to be able to say "amen," which means, "So be it."

Near the end of the 1950s, during some of the most tense years of the Cold War, the Soviet Union beat the U.S. in the race to space.

The outer atmosphere became an ideological battleground, with the two competing worldviews demonstrating their strength. In 1961, Soviet cosmonaut Yuri Gagarin became the first man in space. Later that year, President John F. Kennedy cast a compelling vision that moved the heart of our nation. He boldly proclaimed that he planned "to put a man on the moon by the end of the decade." He would never see that vision come to pass, but he cast it in such a compelling way that it outlasted him. On July 20, 1969, that vision was achieved as Neil Armstrong took "one small step for man, one giant leap for mankind" when he stepped onto the moon's surface. We accomplished this outrageous feat because of a leader who knew how to cast a compelling vision.

Dave and Jon Ferguson's book Exponential: *How to Accomplish the Jesus Mission* describes the compelling nature of big dreams: "Big dreams are also contagious. They are infectious. They not only change you, but they can also slowly begin to change your friends and those around you! Big dreams generate excitement, and they attract those who want to follow your example and step out in faith."[75] Leaders cast a clear, compelling, and infectious vision that will inspire people to action.

A compelling vision creates action. Hybels explains the relationship of vision and action in the church: "Vision is the fuel that leaders run on. It's the energy that creates action. It's the fire that ignites the passion of followers. It's the clear call that sustains focused effort year after year, decade after decade, as people offer consistent and sacrificial service to God."[76] Why do so many established churches succumb to an ingrown focus? They do so because they lack a clear and compelling vision of the future.

A Sneak Peek on Vision Casting

Vision casting is better caught than taught. I love watching great leaders cast vision. Anytime I can get around a leader who either purposefully or even accidentally casts a compelling vision, I am all ears.

May I take a moment to provide one example of how I cast vision? I purposefully paint a picture of the role of our church in reaching people for Christ, and the kind of church I want New Life to be. I work hard to create potent imagery in the minds and hearts of the people of New Life. Such vision casting typically comes during or at the end of a message. I often begin to talk about some fictional people choosing this weekend to visit New Life. For example:

> For a moment, New Life, I want to introduce you to a young wife who has a husband who is far from God and disinterested in the claims of Christ. This wife has been attending New Life for a couple of years now, unfortunately without her husband. She is thirty-two years old and has been married for five years. She has two kids, a three-year-old and a newborn.
>
> Let me tell you a little of her story. She married a guy who had little interest in religion, but she hoped that after marriage he would attend church with her one day. You know how this story goes; we all have seen it way too many times. They got married. Had kids. Got caught up with working jobs and keeping the bills paid. Went into debt. And the American Dream lives on . . .
>
> She decided a few years ago to start attending church. Typically, he refuses to come. She takes the kids anyway while he enjoys watching football by himself. Honestly, she had almost given up on him. But for some reason, out of the blue, today he decided to come to church. His decision shocked her. She had no idea why this Sunday would be the day he would choose to join her and the kids at church.
>
> She feels very nervous about his first visit. Everything in her wants her husband to like the church enough to perhaps come back. She gets up early to make sure all the kids are ready. She knows that her husband will use any

excuse to get out of church. Finally, they all get in the car. As they drive up to the parking lot, she prays for a good parking spot. She just hopes to see normal-looking parking lot attendants today. She hopes that he feels good about this church the moment they drive up and doesn't find an excuse to turn around.

The first thing that needs to happen is to get the kids checked into the nursery. As she walks up to the nursery, she talks to herself under her breath: "I just hope the nursery workers are all there and ready to check in the kids." She prays that they are in a good mood, not griping about a lack of volunteers.

Then the moment of truth . . . she walks into the lobby with her husband. She looks around, she praying that someone doesn't "attack" him and make him feel uncomfortable. All she wants is some guy who can talk sports with him and connect with her husband. Then she walks into the auditorium.

There she stands in church with her husband. She holds her breath. She wants only for the music to connect with her husband (and that no weird stuff happens in the service). She knows one small thing can ruin this moment for her husband.

Then the pastor stands up to preach. Her prayer at this moment: "Don't let this be the day where we talk about tithing or politics." She hopes her husband will connect with the style of the pastor and connect in a meaningful way.

She prays that her husband will connect at this church.

She prays that her kids will love the kids' ministry.

She prays that God will transform her husband and he will surrender his life to Christ.

This is our vision for this church. Your friends, your spouse, and your kids need a place they can belong, a place to discover the claims of Christ and become a fully devoted follower of Jesus Christ.

Our vision is to be a church that unchurched people can attend. A church that will answer the prayers of this wife. A church where you can invite people far from God, and together we can see Jesus transform our lives.

A church where everything we do, from the parking lot to children's ministry, in the lobby and in our gatherings, will become a part of someone's salvation story. This is our vision. Every weekend, people are having the courage to invite someone who is far from God to come and experience an authentic environment where they can begin their salvation story.

It's almost impossible to describe in writing my tone of voice and cadence. But try to feel the power of the vision in this narraphor. The audience leans in. The people laugh at appropriate moments. They begin to "see" their roles in helping someone find Jesus. And they think: *This is attainable! This is believable! This is compelling!*

At the risk of sounding redundant, I want to emphasize that an attainable, believable, and compelling vision *must come from God.* Every gripping vision for the church ultimately comes from God. This is why I asked the two pivotal questions in chapter 1:

What is God birthing in your heart?

What is your providential assignment for this local church?

At the end of the day, these are the only questions that really matter. It is this kind of vision that will become a catalyst for meaningful and irresistible change in your church.

Coaching Assignments

1. Think of your church three years from now. Start painting a picture of the future you see. What does your church look like in thirty-six months? Draw it out on a napkin. What is your vision?

2. Think of someone who truly knows how to cast vision. What is true about this person? How does he or she cast vision in such a way that moves the organization forward?

3. Find an environment where you can cast vision to a group of people. As you prepare to cast this vision, ask yourself:

   • Is it attainable?

   • Is it believable?

   • Is it compelling?

Part Four

THE RELAUNCH PHASE:
STOP TINKERING WITH CHANGE AND DO IT

The final stage of the Recalibration Dance is the Relaunch Phase, where leaders stop tinkering with change and do it. This is where a leader hits the tarmac and does three practical things:

- Date it.
- Define it.
- Do it.

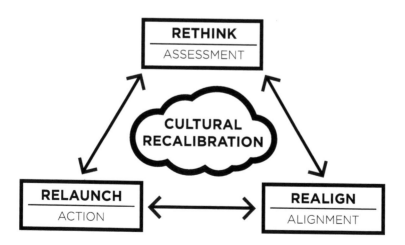

This is the time for action. It's the time to pull the trigger, the time to hit the tarmac, the time to stop tinkering with change and do it.

It is time for your church to experience a divine tipping point where everything changes. This is the moment of critical mass, the threshold, the boiling point for your church to experience a cultural recalibration.

In part 4, we'll cover the final three (of nine) Relaunch Practices:

- *Practice #7* | Relaunch with Courage: Talk is Cheap
- *Practice #8* | Hit the Tarmac! Date It. Define It. Do It.
- *Practice #9* | Make Continuous Improvements: Progress, Not Perfection

You will never learn how to dance without moving your feet, without getting out on the dance floor and actually dancing. You can read books all day about dancing. You can watch videos and even practice. But at some point, the music will turn on and you need to dance.

I practiced and practiced for the big moment of the father-daughter dance at my daughter's wedding. When the DJ finally said, "It's time for the daddy-daughter dance," I felt nervous. It took every ounce of courage inside of me . . . but I did it! I danced.

Relaunching your church is all about action. So date it. Define it. And then do it.

11

PRACTICE #7
RELAUNCH WITH COURAGE:
Talk Is Cheap

There is no painless way to put this: at some point, leaders have to stop talking about change and do it.

You have to take action. You have to pull the trigger. You have to reach deep inside of you and cry out to God for the courage to relaunch.

This is the tipping point, the threshold, the boiling point—when everything can change in almost the blink of an eye. When the leader is born!

Patrick and DeVine express what is required in leadership if we want God to do something inexplicable: "In every kingdom endeavor, there is a time and a place for raw faith. A time to risk comfort, security, and all you have known for the reward of seeing God do something unexplainable."[76]

> There is no painless way to put this: at some point, leaders have to stop talking about change and do it.

Do you want to see God do something inexplicable in your church? Then you have to step out in faith and relaunch.

The Biggest Load-Bearing Wall

When I became the lead pastor of New Life, one of the first staff hires I had to make was a worship leader. I quickly ran into one of the biggest load-bearing walls of New Life. Would I choose the kind of worship leader I felt God leading me to, or would I hire a worship leader who could lead a choir and orchestra in the current music style of the church?

To further complicate matters, everyone seemed to want my wife, a gifted worship leader in her own right, to lead worship. But both of us knew and agreed that the direction of worship culture at New Life did not match her gift mix. So again: what would I do?

At first, I tried to blend the worship cultures. But when I interviewed twenty worship leaders, I quickly ran into a serious problem: every worship leader with whom I resonated lacked the skills, passion, or expertise to lead a choir and orchestra. I didn't see how I could achieve that blend. I desperately wanted to incorporate the choir and orchestra, but after many sleepless nights and turmoil, I knew I had to decide. Would I hire a worship pastor whom I knew would resonate with the culture I believed God wanted me to cultivate, or would I hire someone who knew how to lead a choir and orchestra? I could not do both.

For me, it was three years of turmoil and all-out hell. I didn't know it back then, but looking back, I see I was making one of the most mission-critical, load-bearing choices of my leadership.

To understand the tension I felt, some backstory might help. As I mentioned in chapter 7, our church over the years had become known for its choir and orchestra productions. Back in the '80s, we had an incredible Singing Christmas Tree program. God used this outreach to touch the lives of thousands of people in our area. Our music ministry was vital to the soul of the church.

I knew that if we made this change, we would lose people. How many? I didn't know for sure, but it scared me. Everything inside of me wanted to keep our choir and orchestra, but I knew deep down inside that the environments we needed to create on Sunday and the new style of music wouldn't allow it. Still, I kept delaying and compromising the decision. I kept trying to say, "Let's have the choir and orchestra twice a month, then once a month, and then seasonally."

I was the problem! I lacked courage to make the decision. I didn't want to pay the price of change. Because of my lack of courage, people began thinking I was lying to them. I started to lose credibility because I lacked the courage to make a tough decision.

Finally my wife said to me, "Pull the trigger! Stop tinkering with change and do it!" And so we started the process of recalibrating our music and worship at New Life.

It was a brutal time. I remember our final meeting of the choir and orchestra as if it happened only yesterday. It felt like a funeral. The raw emotions of people in pain caused them to say things that deeply hurt. I still feel the pain as I write this chapter.

An Honest Confession

I sometimes delay launching new initiatives or making needed changes for too long because I don't like losing people. Especially if they are tithers—that's right, I said it. This is my fallen humanity. When people leave the church, it feels quite personal, and it affects me deeply. I hate it.

Every time I make any significant decision or lead my church in a relaunch or change initiative, a certain amount of stress and fear haunts me. Every time I recalibrate and make any kind of change initiative, I feel scared to death and full of doubts and questions.

Will this work?

Will I lose good people from my church?

Will this work over time?

How do we pay for this?

If we add a new service, will anyone show up?

If I attempt to rethink or relaunch my church, will this fall on deaf ears?

Every time, I have to search deep down inside of me and ask God for the courage to move forward. Courage is acting and moving forward despite fear and insecurity. Leadership is not about totally overcoming fear; sometimes it is simply about moving forward.

Relaunching your church or organization will take the kind of courage that comes only from God.

It will take:

- Courage to admit your church or organization needs to rethink everything
- Courage to ask probing and piercing questions
- Courage to define what is mission critical and what is not
- Courage to cast a new vision to the church
- Courage to believe God for new ground, new ministries, and new momentum
- Courage to accept that some people won't like you or your new ideas
- Courage to set a precise date and then announce that date

I don't care how much a church prays, seeks advice, reads, or educates itself; it takes courage to forge new ground for the Kingdom of God. You may have all the best ideas and God-inspired plans for your church, but without exercising courage, a congregation will never move forward.

There is no doubt that you *will* face dark days as you relaunch your church. People *will* say things about you and to you that will hurt. You *will* lose some people from your church. You may even have to take a couple steps backward to move forward.

This is why you need to know that you know you have heard from God. At times, the leader will stand alone as he or she makes decisions that seem risky or even hurtful to the people around them.

Leadership demands courage.

Courage Versus Stupidity

Courage and stupidity are not the same thing. Courage is doing what you know God has told you to do. Stupidity often means acting on some crazy idea despite the counsel and wisdom of others.

> Courage is acting and moving forward despite fear and insecurity.

It is easy to get the notion that courageous leaders are like Superman, other worldly beings that are "faster than a speeding bullet, more powerful than a locomotive, able to leap tall buildings in a single bound!" This may work well in a comic book universe, but it doesn't play out well in wise leadership.

We think courageous leadership is for leaders who are naturally bold, love risk, and live to put everything on the line. But it simply isn't true.

It might help to ponder several principles that can strengthen leaders to pull the trigger and make a decision. At first glance, these realities may seem counterintuitive to courage. But the truth is that learning these secrets is basic to leading with courage. Consider a few foundational truths that will help you to move forward.

1. Leaders take calculated risks

Perhaps one of the greatest secrets of courageous leadership is that leaders take calculated risks and not reckless risks. A calculated risk is one that the leader studies and considers before taking. Leaders consider whether this change is mission critical or merely important, load bearing or non-load bearing. Leaders weigh all the possible outcomes and potential impacts of a decision and then choose the consequences that they can live with. Calculated risks weigh the likely gains against the probable losses, and effective leaders choose the potential gain over the potential loss.

In his work *Innovation's Dirty Little Secret*, Osborne discusses how innovators exhibit a unique form of courage, one that differs from the kind of courage most might anticipate: "It's not the wild risk-taking kind of courage that you might expect. They don't take crazy and wild risks. Instead, they take carefully calculated risks."[78]

Leaders need wisdom and knowledge to truly calculate any risk. I often pray a prayer first spoken by King Solomon. When God told him he could have anything his heart desired, Solomon prayed, "Give me wisdom and knowledge, that I may lead this people, for who is able to govern this great people of yours?" (2 Chronicles 1:10). I pray, "God, give me wisdom and knowledge when it comes to the timing of change, seasons of change, and my personal leadership capital to lead the change." I recommend the same prayer to you.

2. Leaders learn from setbacks and misfires

One unspoken reason leaders don't recalibrate their churches is fear of failure. Dave and Jon Ferguson provide good insight into why so many churches get stuck in the status quo: "There is a fear of failure that hinders churches from taking risk. We say to ourselves, 'I'm afraid it just won't work and I can't accept the possibility of failure.' We work for years to build a large church or successful career, and our 'success' can become the very thing that gets in the way of our taking more significant risks. We tell ourselves, 'I've accomplished too much to lose it all.'"[79]

Most leaders have a defective understanding of the word "failure." I personally define it like this: "setbacks or misfires that all high-capacity leaders will naturally face at some time." I have learned over the years that setbacks and misfires are normal and that not every decision (or change) brings overwhelming success. Mistakes and missteps will happen and are to be to be expected in leadership.

Leadership is all about understanding setbacks and misfires, an inherent part of leadership. Leaders must have the courage and grace to look at these events and reflect on the lessons learned. They then should use this reflection as a way to grow in leadership, not allowing it to prevent them from moving forward.

Here is the untold truth of leadership that most leaders avoid discussing: nearly *all* innovation and change initiatives, at some point, suffer setbacks and misfires. Osborne provides the dirty little secret to innovation: "It's simply this: most innovations fail. It doesn't matter whether we're talking about a new product, a new program, or a new process. It can be a new company or even a new church. When it comes time to start something new or make a major change, the surest horse you can bet on is the one called Failure."[80]

> One unspoken reason leaders don't recalibrate their churches is fear of failure.

So how can you more effectively deal with failure, with the setbacks and misfires you will inevitably suffer?

Let me offer a few suggestions:

View setbacks and misfires through a biblical lens. This is where theology and Scripture give me great help. Think about all the times that leaders in Scripture endured setbacks and misfires. David did not allow his sin to disrupt his rule as king. Jonah ran from the call of God, only to return. Peter moved past his denial of Christ to become a pillar of the early church. A look at Hebrews 11 will reveal a list of spiritual giants who all faced setbacks and misfires.

Looking at these stories of failure remind me of a crucial reality in leadership. Because we have eternal goals, and because God is perpetually working all things together for our good, failure is never final. Failure then becomes a learning tool that drives the leader forward to the next initiative. Failure becomes final only when the leader gives up and decides to quit leading.

View setbacks and misfires as a well-earned education. Some of us have a doctorate in setbacks and misfires. This is both normal and healthy. View them as a well-earned education. I learned my greatest lessons not in my victories, but in my failures.

I love how Walter Brunell reframes failure: "Failure is the tuition you pay for success."[81] Leadership does not worry about avoiding failure at any cost. It rather seeks to learn, grow, and get back up from failure. Leaders need to learn to fail fast, fail forward, and even fail sideways.

> Mistakes and missteps will happen and are to be to be expected in leadership.

Helio Fred Garcia has spent more than thirty years helping leaders build trust, inspire loyalty, and lead more effectively. In the anthology *Building Success with Business Ethics: Advice from Business Leaders*, he tells a fictional story about legendary IBM CEO, Thomas Watson. A high-potential junior manager reputedly made a mistake that cost IBM $5 million dollars. Devastated by his error, the junior executive offered his resignation, but Watson would not accept it. Confused, the young man said, "I don't understand. I made a terrible mistake. Why on earth would you want to keep me?" Watson replied, "I just invested $5 million on your learning curve. Why would I want to waste that kind of money?"[82]

View setbacks and misfires as steps in the right direction, not as dead ends. Leaders often use the phrase, "Failure is not final." I go a step beyond this and say, "Failure is a step in the right direction." I know this is easier said than done! Thomas Edison failed countless times while inventing all sorts of products, including the light bulb and the storage battery. His authorized biography, *Edison: His Life and Inventions*, quotes friend and associate Walter S. Mallory about the inventor's struggles to develop working prototypes of things we take for granted today:

> This had been going on more than five months, seven days a week, when I was called down to the laboratory to see him [Edison]. I found him at a bench about three feet wide and twelve feet long, on which there were hundreds of little test cells that had been made up by his corps of chemists and experimenters. I then learned that he had thus made over nine thousand experiments in trying to devise this new type of storage battery, but had not produced a single thing that promised to solve the question. In view of this immense amount of thought and labor, my sympathy got the better of my judgment, and I said: "Isn't it a shame that with the tremendous amount of work you have done you haven't been able to get any results?" Edison turned on me like a flash, and with a smile replied: "Results! Why, man, I have gotten lots of results! I know several thousand things that won't work!"[83]

In many ways, recalibrating your church is an experiment in what won't work. You *will* fail. But consider every failure as a step toward your church moving forward. I once heard a church leader put it this way: "We never say something has failed; we say only that the experiment has run its course."

Leaders make mid-course corrections. Amazon has become one of the biggest retailers in the world. Jeff Bezos, the founder of Amazon. com, has noted that people who are right a lot of the time are the same people who change their minds a lot of the time, especially when the facts prove them wrong.[84] Leaders have the courage and humility to change their minds. They plan in pencil and refuse to get stubborn.

One of the secrets to leading with courage is refusing to get stubborn and being willing to make mid-course corrections. Often, we think that leaders who change their minds or make a mid-course corrections lack courage. Quite the opposite! Leaders willingly change their minds when they receive new, contradictory data or when the results they expected to see just don't materialize. It takes courage and humility to make a necessary mid-course correction.

During every recalibration, you will have to make mid-course adjustments. Something won't work as you planned. You will get disappointed from time to time. When that happens, make adjustments, but don't lose heart! Your goal is not to get everything perfect; your goal is to recalibrate your church, challenge the status quo, create a new cultural norm, and get the church back on mission. Your goal is to infuse new cultural DNA into your church. Your goal is to create a new operating system in the fabric of your church that enables you to fulfill your God-inspired vision.

My Most Courageous Decision

As a fairly new lead pastor at New Life, I had to plan the construction of a new building, a dream that had lived in the heart of New Life since the '80s. We met in a multi-purpose room that the school used as a gym during the week.

I cast a clear and compelling vision for rebuilding the entire church, including a kids' ministry area, dead center in our parking lot instead of adding on to our current building.

I built my vision on some solid reasoning:

- People would have better parking closer to the church.
- The church would become more visible from the street.
- It would allow for dedicated space for all of our ministries.
- It would help facilitate our Christian school.

We created a website to promote the vision, created a virtual tour of the new building, and raised money to construct the facility, complete with full architectural plans. I cast the vision, I leveraged all my leadership capital, and we held a month of meetings at my house to communicate the vision.

I certainly had a clear and compelling vision. The people believed it. But it wasn't attainable for us. We quickly got sticker shock! We simply lacked the finances to build an entirely new building in the middle of our parking lot. The price would have been two and half times the cost of what I'd expected. To further complicate matters, when the capital campaign pledges came in, we had just half of what I'd hoped for.

I felt devastated. And I found myself in a great dilemma.

I found myself up against what I considered the most courageous decision I had ever made. I knew the vision was from God—but somehow I needed to go back to the drawing board. For two weeks, I walked around in a fog. For the first time in my life, I felt paralyzed; I simply didn't know what to do.

How would I stand in front of my church and tell them I made a mistake? That the dream I had cast was impossible for us and would never happen? How could I justify the money I had just spent on the construction plans? Was it all one huge waste?

The most courageous decision I made was an internal one. I had to be willing to back up, return to the drawing board, and rethink our entire building plans. It took internal resolve.

I remember standing with one of my leaders, who said, "Why not build a new auditorium right beside the current church, and use the current auditorium for your children's ministry?"

We had an incredible building that I had intended to abandon. Why not instead turn it into the children's and school facilities? Practically, this would mean building a 35,000-square-foot facility instead of a 75,000-square-foot facility. Also, our kids' ministry would have a much larger space available to them than the one I wanted to build.

I knew it would be complicated to build in this location because of wetland setbacks required by the county, and because of a hillside behind the original building (that's what made us think about building in the center of the parking lot in the first place). A novice leader might have said, "Have the courage to overbuild and overspend on this project!" But a courageous leader says, "Have the courage to admit you were wrong and go back to the drawing board."

This setback and misfire on my part would prove to be a step in the right direction, not a dead end—although it was also a very expensive education. We had already spent lots of our available funds on building plans. I could have looked at this mistake and the cost of architectural plans as a waste of money, or as a very expensive education. Thank God the board and the church allowed this to be a part of the learning curve of my leadership!

To make a long story short, I quickly discovered that our county would be almost impossible to work with on the expansion. We therefore had to do something very courageous: stop the entire process and annex into the city of Renton. That took a whole year! It was both risky and courageous, but I considered it a calculated risk. After twelve months of continual work, we finally got annexed into the city of Renton, where the setback and wetland issues were minor compared to King County.

I now see this as God's protection on me and on New Life. Building in the middle of the parking lot would have paralyzed the future of our church. Our original design called for a kids' space that would quickly have proven too small. We could not have managed the enormous mortgage. We would have found it impossible to hold services during construction because of parking.

I thank God that He gave me the courage to make a calculated rather than a reckless risk, to learn from my setback and misfire, and to make a mid-course correction. This one act of courage saved New Life millions of dollars.

Be Strong and Courageous

When God gave Joshua the task of leading the Israelites into the Promised Land, the Lord told him, "Be strong and courageous. Do not be afraid; do not be discouraged, for the Lord your God will be with you wherever you go" (Joshua 1:9).

Be strong! Be courageous! Why? God will be with you wherever you go.

The very fact that you have reached this point in the book tells me that you are the type of leader who is ready to truly lead your church in a cultural change. I'm glad, because your church is worth recalibrating. Your people need a leader to stand and lead, a leader who is unafraid to challenge the status quo.

Yes, there will be sleepless nights. People will question your motives. You will lose people you love dearly. Others will say unfair things about you.

But the future of your church is at stake. The souls of men and women on their way to hell hang in the balance. You can't stay in the desert forever. You have to move forward with courage and strength.

Now is the time.

Coaching Assignments

1. What fears do you have about relaunching your church? Be honest. Write them down.

2. What misconceptions do many leaders have about courage?

3. Pray for courage. Ask God to infuse you with the type of courage that comes only from heaven.

12

PRACTICE #8
HIT THE TARMAC:
Date It. Define It. Do It.

In this chapter, I will hit the tarmac with you. Here, we want to get practical and bring the entire book together in a way that helps you recalibrate your church.

It's possible you skipped the rest of this book and decided to read this single chapter alone. I know many leaders like the practical stuff and prefer to disregard transferable principles and practices (as outlined in the other chapters). I get this and understand the temptation. I have done this myself, far too often.

But with that said, such an approach explains why attempts at recalibrating established churches fail so often. There are no shortcuts! And so I encourage you to resist the temptation to speed-read the book.

Recalibration is not an event, campaign, or program. Don't ignore the underlying assumptions, culture, and practices. You must carefully think through the critical phases and practices of recalibration if you are to succeed.

Effective leaders know how to think at 30,000 feet *and* hit the tarmac at the same time. Good leaders know how to be a visionary and execute at the same time. At one moment, leaders are talking about vision, mission, and philosophy; in the next, they are discussing some of the most practical, mission-critical issues in the organization.

Think about flying a plane. No competent pilot would consider it a success to take off, complete the journey, and then fly around the tarmac. A flight succeeds only once it lands. While I believe there may be good reasons for holding patterns in decision-making, at some point a leader must hit the tarmac and land the plane. Otherwise, he or she will have a planeload of frustrated, disgruntled passengers.

Stop tinkering with change and start leading change.

A Few Things Before You Start

Before you hit the tarmac, I want to encourage you to do a few things. We've already talked about all of them. Make sure you don't skip over any of these vital steps.

1. Hear from God

Before you relaunch your church, you need to hear from God. You need a divine assignment from God and God alone. Your motivation has to come from a heavenly calling and not merely a craving for the temporary results of numerical growth. Get away for a personal retreat. Something happens when you take a few days to get away and hear from God.

2. Treat your church like an owner, not a renter

Years ago, I felt deeply frustrated with the lack of progress I saw at New Life. I wanted the changes to happen much more quickly. Dary Northrop, pastor of Timberline Church in Colorado, was coaching me. He asked me during one call, "Do you treat your church like an owner or a renter?" The question caught me completely by surprise.

I have renters. I know how many treat their stuff. Renters can leave at any moment and so tend not to take good care of the house. Owners, on the other hand, are committed. They tend to take far better care of the house.

This is the time to put a stake in the ground as it relates to your church. Own the condition of your church. Own the vision. Own the future of your church. If you do not feel ready to commit to your church for the next three to five years, both emotionally and spiritually, then I encourage you to forget about recalibrating the congregation.

Are you truly committed for the long haul to remain at your church? Or are you just waiting for the next opportunity? Are you acting like an owner or a renter?

Do you feel called by God to lead this particular congregation into a culture of recalibration? Are you ready to see your church have full Kingdom impact in its community and world?

"Do you treat your church like an owner or a renter?"

3. Make sure this is about God's Kingdom and not yours

We all wrestle with inner motives. Why do we want the church to grow? Is this about numbers or truly transformed lives? Am I really stirred by the Great Commission, or do I just want to be recognized publicly for some false notion of growth?

I can't say all my motives are pure. I am not sure that any of us can. My humanity is real, just like yours. I like large numbers and pats on the back, just like everyone else. Every leader likes those things.

But we Christian leaders must do some honest soul-searching. We need to somehow go deeper than numbers or growth for the sake of growth. Such shallow incentives will never sustain you through the turbulence of change. We need to be compelled and consumed by the Great Commission. We need to be committed to building God's Kingdom, not ours.

4. Begin to ask yourself some probing and piercing questions

Take some time to ask yourself some personal, gut-level questions. Get a journal and write down your reflections.

Ask yourself:

- What is God birthing in my heart?
- What is bugging me about my church? What makes me cringe?
- How can our church reach its full Kingdom impact?

In appendix C, I provide some probing and piercing questions from visionary leaders across the nation. Pick three to five of these, get alone, and begin to wrestle with what you believe God may be birthing in your heart.

5. Get outside perspective

As we saw in chapter 4, most of us need outside perspective to discover what God is really speaking to us. In the ministry world, we tend to underestimate the power of fresh eyes. The truth is that most of us have grown so used to our own "smell" that we need outside perspective. Get fresh eyes. I know this may cost time and money, but do it anyway.

6. Learn the story of your church

Some of the hints and secrets to recalibrating your church lie in the stories of your church. In many ways, recalibration is about returning to the original settings of your church.

Recapture the values deeply embedded in the story of your church. Take some time to read the minutes of your church meetings and any historical documents. Interview three to five people with a long history at the church and ask about the values that started the church. Learn the stories of your church. All of this information will be vital as you recalibrate.

7. Get ready to stretch every leadership muscle in your body

Your church mirrors your own leadership shape. It is time for you to stretch every leadership muscle in your body. Read through the nine practices outlined in this book, but do more than just read about them—practice them. Practice them like someone on a workout schedule. Do three sets of twelve. When you stretch these leadership muscles, you will feel pain—but this kind of pain is good. It means you are stretching. My trainer yells at me and says, "Power through!" Don't cheat on the last set. Those last few reps stretch the muscles and build muscle mass.

Relaunch Initiative: Date It. Define It. Do It.

As we saw in chapter 3, the vehicle for recalibrating your church is what I refer to as the Relaunch Initiative. This is a time-bound, well-defined and mission-critical initiative that serves as a catalyst to recalibrate your church. The Relaunch Initiative helps your church gain full Kingdom impact.

Think like a church planter. One of the first things a church planter does is to set the launch date of the new church. From that date, they work backwards. Everything is built around this date.

Next, they begin to define what the church will look like. Church planters understand the huge work involved. They have no choice but to actually do it, or the church won't open. When a team plants a new church, they talk about it, tell all their friends and family, determine the launch date, go to launch trainings, feel nervous, rally the team, pray, hope people will show up, raise money, beg people to join the team, take risks, and continue to pray like crazy.

You must do the same thing.

Date It

Whenever leaders tell me they want to relaunch a church, I normally ask them, "Okay, *when* will you relaunch your church?" If a Relaunch Initiative is not time bound, it won't work. Until a leader dates it, he or she is not serious about recalibrating the church. Such leaders are still stuck in a philosophical stage, not ready to move the church forward. Now, nothing is wrong with a philosophical conversation. But somewhere along the way, you have to go from philosophical to practical. You have to turn your vision into a reality.

Something happens in the heart of the leader who says, "On this particular day, our church is putting a stake in the ground and believing God to accomplish something great and new in our congregation and our community."

People will look up. They will pay attention. An exact date convinces people that the leader is serious. The date must be precise, exact, and strategic. Until you name a precise date, all you are doing is talking.

Keep three things in mind as you determine this tipping point, the catalytic date- and time-bound initiative for your church:

1. Determine the best time of the year

The best time of the year will vary for every church. Because I am located in Seattle, for example, and New Life is only miles from the

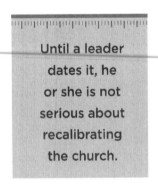

Until a leader dates it, he or she is not serious about recalibrating the church.

Seahawks training facility. I avoid January when doing a Relaunch Initiative. The last several years, the Seahawks have been highly competitive in the NFL playoffs, and people become a little more flexible with their church attendance. I want the largest number of people to hear about what's coming. Also, I find that January is a great time to cast vision and prepare the heart of the church for the vision.

I once made a huge mistake when I did a big change initiative on the day that daylight saving time began. Bad idea! When people lose an hour of sleep, they get cranky.

For us, the best times of the year for recalibrating occur in February (the weekend after the Super Bowl) or later in September

(I actually watch when the fall TV shows are returning and think in terms of those dates).

The Easter season has also been a great time to launch an initiative, as people make their annual visits to church. It provides an opportunity to demonstrate the vitality and excitement that's building in your church.

2. Think in terms of nine months

For significant cultural initiatives, I encourage leaders to think in terms of nine months leading up to the change. Many leaders either rush the process or take far too long, and either extreme will hurt momentum. You don't want your church or your staff to feel rushed in this process. They need time to process and allow the concepts to seep into the culture. On the other hand, you don't want people getting bored and wondering if anything will ever happen.

Nine months is only 270 days. You want a period long enough to allow the change to seep into the culture, and yet short enough for everyone to feel the countdown taking place.

This period passes quickly, but it provides a sense of urgency to not waste a moment. It also provides enough time to allow people to process the change and to actually get the work done.

New Life now has such a culture of recalibration that, at times, we allow only three to five months for this process—but remember, recalibration has become a cultural norm for us. I don't recommend such a short time frame for most churches.

3. Start a countdown clock

I am coaching one pastor who actually put a countdown clock in the main office so everyone can see it every day. This creates momentum, energy, and a sense that "We are all in this together."

Open every conversation with, "In 202 days, God is going to do something very cool at our church," or "In 201 days, this is how our church will look." Cast vision, share your heart, and help your people see what God has put in your spirit.

Define It

You truly hit the tarmac of leadership when you clearly define the Relaunch Initiative. Here, you plainly describe the mission-critical changes for your relaunch. A Relaunch Initiative must be both well defined and mission critical at the same time.

Again, you have to be *clear!* When the leader is vague, people listen (but that's all). When the leader is clear, however, people get things done. It is just that simple.

Such laser-beam clarity will not happen in one conversation. Reaching clarity takes time. Use this time to marinate with your team, board and influencers.

Define and clarify. Create different environments to rethink your church and clearly define what God is saying to you. Get out the whiteboard and ask probing and piercing questions.

Ask for feedback. Pick three to five questions and involve your key influencers in healthy discussion and robust debate. Create environments where your staff can suggest honest ideas and insights without you or others getting defensive.

Put it in writing. The first thing I coach leaders to do in developing a Relaunch Initiative is to put it in writing. By its very nature, writing brings clarity. Create a working document so people can begin to give their input and discuss their ideas. Something powerful happens when the leader writes it down. In Habakkuk 2:2, God says to the prophet regarding the vision in his heart, "Write down the revelation and make it plain on tablets so that a herald may run with it." Your staff, board, influencers, and congregation can't run with your vision if you don't write it down.

Keep it flexible but not fuzzy. When you lead change, you have to know when to pivot and when to stand your ground. I love Osborne's insights on how he presents change to his staff and board: "I always present first drafts, not final proposals. By this, I don't mean that I offer half-baked ideas or suggestions off the top of my head. My first drafts are carefully thought out and persuasively presented. But I don't confuse them with God's final revealed will. That's something the board, staff, and I will determine together."[85]

Seven Elements of a Relaunch Initiative

Leaders must clearly define seven things for a Relaunch Initiative to take hold. All seven elements are necessary to get the blood pumping in their churches and the neurons firing in the brains of their staff.

1. The relaunch name

The name of the Relaunch Initiative is not some shallow exercise. It is how everyone will refer to this initiative and it will, by its very nature, create new culture in your church. You define the culture of the church with its name, much like naming a child. So spend some time on this. Make sure the name resonates deeply with you. I admit this is not my strength, which is probably why New Life tends to use simple, date-based names, such as "2.12.12" or "3.16.16." But they work for us. Under these names, we add a short phrase. For 2.12.12, the phrase was "Everything Changes." For 3.16.16, it was "I See a Church."

On my website, *www.recalibrategroup.com/resources*, I have provided a list of names used by other churches. The name itself should create culture, momentum, and excitement.

2. The relaunch team

Your team will make or break a Relaunch Initiative. Identify who on your team will carry the burden of specific changes you are

> **I have discovered that giving plays a significant role in the church buying into the change initiative.**

making. Who will lead the changes and actually make them happen? At New Life, we call them "champions" of each change initiative.

Each of your staff members needs to champion a particular piece of the Relaunch Initiative. One thing I love about Relaunch Initiatives is that they unite the staff. All your staff will work on one thing together. No silos. No agendas besides the whole church.

Who should be on your relaunch team? Open up your mind to the possibilities.

- Some high-capacity leaders in your congregation would love to be on your relaunch team. Give them specific instructions.
- Involve your spouse. Make sure he or she is engaged on your team.
- You may have an administrative person who can carry the burden of some specific piece of this Relaunch Initiative.

3. The relaunch scope

The relaunch scope defines exactly what mission-critical changes you will make in this specific timeframe. You can't change everything. You must think mission critical! Don't waste your energy on changes that won't move your church forward.

The precise scope of the Relaunch Initiative is critical. Here, you define the scorecard and put together your metrics of change. You need to consider finances, the story of the church, your leadership capital, and the emotional bandwidth of the church.

You can typically break these down into five to seven major categories and then create sub-points under each one. The sub-points can contain the substance that will help move the church forward. I have found that three of them often become the driving force behind cultivating momentum in your church.

4. The relaunch financial plan

A lot of Relaunch Initiatives fail because leaders don't do their financial homework. Leaders must carefully think through the finances.

This is a great time to call your church to generous giving. I have discovered that giving plays a significant role in the church buying into the change initiative. Your church will give to vision. Just as you would never build a new facility without raising funds or plant a new church without asking people to give, when you recalibrate your church, you have to call your people to put their money where their mouth is.

5. The relaunch communication plan

Develop a well-thought-out communication plan of the vision and Relaunch Initiative. Utilize all available resources to communicate the Relaunch Initiative to your church.

- Utilize social media (Twitter, Facebook, Instagram)
- Create videos that can stir vision in your congregation
- Creative signage and branding
- Cast vision during your message
- Do a "Save the Date" three months ahead of time
- Email blast
- Website
- Have every ministry department build excitement within their tribe (children, youth, young adults, small groups, production, etc.)

6. The relaunch timeline

The relaunch timeline starts with the precise relaunch date. Once you have set this date, work backwards. On your timeline, you need to identify:

- When things will get done
- When you will communicate each phase to your church
- When you will raise the funds
- When you will launch the initiatives

7. The relaunch day

Plan big for the day you plan to relaunch your church. Make this special. Again, think like a church planter: Signs in the parking lot. Going nuts on social media. Inviting people to be a part of this great moment in your church. Encouraging members of your congregation to invite others to be a part. Bringing in special speakers.

Do It (Last Ninety Days)

By this point, you must feel the urgency. All you should be doing in the last ninety days is working, talking about, and executing the Relaunch Initiative.

When a plane takes off, it can use up to 25 percent of its fuel. I would encourage you to dedicate 20 to 25 percent of your time to this Relaunch Initiative during the last ninety days. Consider seven things that should consume your time during the last ninety days.

1. Make daily progress

During the last ninety days, your goal is to work the plan. Make daily progress. The first thing in the morning, both you and your relaunch team should wake up and ask yourselves, "What will we do today to move the ball forward? We have ninety days remaining; what do we need to do today to make sure we prepare to relaunch this church?"

I cannot overemphasize this part. Your relaunch team needs to dedicate 20 to 25 percent of their time to work the plan during the last ninety days. Everyone needs to free up his or her calendar. Just as a pregnant mother prepares vigorously during the last trimester and a church planter works ceaselessly during the last three months, so you must feel this momentum and free up your calendar.

2. Establish weekly relaunch meetings

During the last ninety days of your Relaunch Initiative, you should hold weekly staff meetings to keep everyone on track and the ball moving forward. The truth is that 20 to 25 percent of your conversations around the office during the day need to be about your Relaunch Initiative.

The authors of 4 *Disciplines of Execution* discuss the "cadence of accountability," which is essential as you lead your organization into its own "wildly important goals." They describe this cadence of accountability as "a rhythm of regular and frequent meetings of any team that owns a wildly important goal. These meetings happen at least weekly and ideally last no more than twenty to thirty minutes. In that brief time, team members hold each other accountable for producing results, despite the whirlwind."[86]

During the last ninety days, I meet weekly with my staff to discuss progress, updates, and the hurdles we face. We do this during our regular staff meetings. While we may discuss other things, the number one thing is the Relaunch Initiative. The synergy and momentum that builds is incredible.

3. Call the church to prayer and fasting

At the end of the day, God is the only one who can recalibrate your church. This is why the church's leader must hear from God. This is why we must ground everything we do in Scripture. Boldly call your church to a focused period of fasting and prayer.

As I write this, New Life is thirteen days from our latest initiative, called 3.16.16 "I See A Church." I am on the Daniel fast, eating only vegetables and fruit. I can't begin to tell you how this is transforming me personally and getting me ready to lead the church into a new season of momentum and Kingdom impact!

4. Infuse new cultural language into your church

When you recalibrate your church, you must create a new lexicon for your congregation to learn and use, which must be infused into everyday language. Some of this will happen as you go, and some of this you need to carefully think through. Create new phrases and words that describe the new cultural operating systems you are plugging into the church. Start using this language.

- Celebrate short-term wins during your last ninety days.
- Tell stories of changed lives. Report wins that God is creating in the church.
- Cast clear vision. Don't be afraid to go on record as to what you are believing God for. Make sure your vision is attainable, believable, and compelling.
- Tell the story of your church. During your preaching, share some of the great stories of sacrifice and dedication in your church's history. Find the stories that illustrate the mission, core values, and vision of your church. Tell those stories to embed them in the future of your church.
- Preach the purpose and mission of the church. Do a preaching series that allows the pastor to share his heart and passion about this local body of Christ.

5. Cross the finish line

As I write, I still have vivid memories of the Seahawks in Super Bowl 2015. Tied 14–14 at halftime, the Seahawks ended the third quarter with a 10-point lead. In the last two minutes, however, the New England Patriots went ahead 28–24.

As the clock wound down to :00, the Seahawks were one yard away from winning the Super Bowl for the second year in a row. Seattle attempted a pass play, which was intercepted at the one-yard line.

So close to winning, and yet they lost. For all their planning and strategy, they couldn't move the ball one yard.

Many leaders make the same mistake. They put great plans and strategies together, but they fail to make the plays that matter most.

Expect Turbulence, Setbacks, and Misfires

Prepare yourself as you hit the tarmac—you *will* have turbulence, setbacks, and misfires. But don't let these discourage you. Get backup! Remember, you may not achieve every goal you set. The key is for you to inspire new excitement, new energy, and move the mission forward in your church. Your goal is for your church to reach its full kingdom impact, not every particular initiative you set out to accomplish.

I meet so many leaders who are cowards when it comes to turbulence or setbacks. They give up. They walk away from the dream.

Expect turbulence! It is normal and to be expected. It's time to say "Game On!" It's time for your church to have full Kingdom impact in your community and the world.

Coaching Assignments

1. Get away for a few days to hear from God. Begin to write down what you believe He may be speaking to you.

2. When will you relaunch your church? Date it.

3. Look carefully at the seven elements of a Relaunch Initiatives. Begin to write out your Relaunch Initiative. Define it.

13

PRACTICE #9
MAKE CONTINUOUS IMPROVEMENTS:
Progress, Not Perfection

This final leadership practice may seem so simple that many will miss it. You may even feel tempted to pass it by. Don't!

Once you relaunch your church, you will start asking the same question that virtually every leader asks me: "Now what?" Your Relaunch Initiative will give your church some new momentum. The people will seem very excited. But then what?

At the root of this question lies the real problem. So often, leaders want quick-fix solutions rather than deep, cultural change. Asking "Now what?" reveals that they are thinking of short-term patches instead of cultural changes.

In fact, the real work begins *after* your Relaunch Initiative.

A Quick Review

For a moment, I want to go full circle with you. I started this book by describing that the culture of recalibration is reflected in two very specific cycles.

Let's review them quickly:

1. Cultural, holistic recalibration (every 3 to 5 years)

Leaders must intentionally and carefully recalibrate their churches every three to five years. As we saw in chapter 1, cultural, holistic recalibration refers to an analysis of the whole instead of a separation into parts. It involves a thorough reexamination of the ministry from the ground up followed by making changes in line with the analysis.

2. Continuous, specific recalibration (all the time)

Continuous recalibration refers to significant adjustments and improvements to specific ministries, practices, and systems within the church. I use the word "continuous" because it implies "never stopping, without interruption, unceasing, and ongoing." Recalibration must happen.

This diagram illustrates the difference between these two types of recalibration.

Cultural Recalibration	Continuous Recalibration
➤ Every 3 to 5 years	➤ All the time
➤ Holistic	➤ Specific
➤ Relaunches the church	➤ Fine-tunes the church
➤ Transforms the culture	➤ Cultivates the culture
➤ Rethinks everything	➤ Rethinks a few things
➤ Mission critical	➤ Mission critical
➤ Holistic systems & practices	➤ Specific systems
➤ Catalyst for innovation	➤ Catalyst for progress
➤ Involves everyone	➤ Involves key leaders

My research on the status of established churches in America started with one question from Dr. Alan Johnson, as I described in chapter 1. "What transferable principles are you learning that can help leaders?" he asked me. The first thing that came to mind was continuous improvements, a crucial part of continuous recalibration.

Making continuous improvements, by definition, involves small, incremental, seemingly insignificant, continuous changes in mission-critical/non-load bearing and load bearing areas of your church. Ongoing, uninterrupted, small, incremental changes will infuse a new cultural norm into the heart and soul of your church. The end result is that you will be relaunching ministries, systems, and programs all the time without even knowing it. I have exercised this leadership muscle for three decades.

Greg Wingard, leadership strategist and founder of Red Bucket Strategies in Kirkland, Washington, introduced me to this concept. I count Greg as one of my lifetime friends. Almost thirty years ago, we were having lunch together as two leaders who wanted to change the world.

"What is the key to great leadership?" I asked him. He looked me in the eye and declared that the key to great leadership is "continuous improvements." He insisted that the key to leadership "is to *never* stop making continuous improvements. Never stop making small, incremental, and continuous improvements."

At that moment, a bell went off in my head. There is no way I could even begin to explain how this one transferable practice has impacted the culture of New Life.

As I write, we are in the middle of a making continuous improvements to our:

- Production department
- Worship culture
- Assimilation process
- Staffing structure
- Youth ministry

The leadership practice of continuous improvements has been the tipping point for New Life to cultivate momentum and stay on mission. It's why you can walk into our door any weekend and experience a church moving forward.

Experience has taught me that in your church, your leadership, and your systems, either you are making continuous improvements or you are experiencing continuous setbacks, every day. Nothing stays the same!

Despite its simple and straightforward appearance, this one leadership practice will create a culture of recalibration in your church and cultivate momentum like nothing else. Best of all, perhaps, no one will ever complain when you practice it.

In fact, very few people will comment on it at all. And yet, over a period of time, these small, incremental, seemingly insignificant, continuous improvements will almost inevitably create a culture of recalibration in your church.

> Experience has taught me that in your church, your leadership, and your systems, either you are making continuous improvements or you are experiencing continuous setbacks, every day.

The Kaizen Way

For years, I had no idea where this phrase "continuous improvements" originated. I eventually discovered that "continuous improvement" is a Japanese concept that comes from the word *kaizen*. The dictionary defines kaizen as "continuous improvement of working practices, personal efficiency, etc., as a business philosophy."[87]

Masaaki Imai first introduced this concept to the West in 1986 in his book *Kaizen: The Key to Japan's Competitive Success*. Recently, he updated his approach in another book titled *Gemba Kaizen*. In this book, he explains the kaizen philosophy:

> In Japanese, *kaizen* means 'continuous improvement.'
> The word implies improvement that involves everyone—

both managers and workers—and entails relatively little expense. The kaizen philosophy assumes that our way of life—be it our working life, our social life, or our home life—should focus on constant improvement efforts. This concept is so natural and obvious to many Japanese that they don't even realize they possess it![88]

The practice of kaizen is foundational for creating a culture of recalibration. Leaders who fail to commit to continuous improvement will never truly develop a strong recalibration culture. Kaizen is embedded in the whole philosophy of recalibration. It's a strong cultural operating system and practice that calls for everyone to make continuous improvements, every day and everywhere.

Everyone makes continuous improvements. Continuous improvements must be a priority for everyone in church leadership, including the pastor, staff, influencers, and board members. Your core leaders and key volunteers must have this mindset. Every volunteer and worker, from production team members to the parking lot attendants, need to be empowered to find and execute continual improvements.

Every day make continuous improvements. Making continuous improvements is not done one day a week, one day a month, or one day a quarter. It is done every day. In every conversation. In every decision. On every Sunday. In every staff meeting.

Everywhere make continuous improvements. Often, we tend to think in terms of only the most obvious areas where continuous improvements need to occur. But continuous improvements need to happen in the parking lot, nursery, kids' environments, and youth environments, in systems behind the scenes, and with volunteers. When I say "everywhere," I speak of a pervasive mentality that understands there is room for improvement in every corner of the church.

Collins' book *Good to Great* transformed the business community. His follow-up book, *Good to Great and the Social Sectors*, is an incredible resource for non-profit companies. As he did in his first book, so Collins uses a metaphor of the flywheel to help readers understand the significance of continuous improvement:

> In building greatness, there is no single defining action, no grand program, no one killer innovation, no solitary lucky break, no miracle moment. Rather, the process resembles relentlessly pushing a giant, heavy flywheel in one direction, turn upon turn, building momentum until a point of breakthrough, and beyond.[89]

Making small, incremental, seemingly insignificant "pushes" on the flywheel of your church will move you forward. Continuous improvements ultimately will cause a catalytic effect in your church. This practice will speed up the rate of your momentum. As the flywheel begins spinning, you will start to feel the march of progress quicken.

Think Progress, Not Perfection

I use the phrase, "progress, not perfection," to communicate what I mean by continuous improvements. On every Sunday and in every message, meeting, and mission-critical area, the goal is to make progress, not achieve perfection.

Perfection is a dauntless and seductive mistress. Perpetually elusive, it forever escapes our grasp while leaving us exhausted in its pursuit. Progress, however, is inherently achievable, simply by improving small details step by step and week to week. Everything can be improved just a little. People can reasonably seek to accomplish just a little more.

If perfection is one of your cultural operating systems, then you will eventually stifle the life out of your board, staff members, influencers, and congregation. This is why I cringe even when someone suggests "excellence" as an organization's cultural norm or core value. In the name of excellence, we cripple the mission of the church, limit those who can serve, and waste resources.

Of course, I believe in excellence. In specific areas, some people would even call me a perfectionist. But neither perfection nor excellence is our mission statement. These cultural operating systems can paralyze an entire church or staff. The real goal is to move the mission forward. The goal is progress, not perfection.

Some leaders paralyze their organizations if they don't have all the answers or lack the energy or capacity to do the job "perfectly." But you can't wait for the perfect conditions to make continuous improvements. You have to make them *today*. So many leaders suffer from a fatal disease called analysis paralysis. They over-analyze or over-think their situations and so never take action.

Organized Chaos

Many leaders ask me, "Once you create a culture of recalibration, how does one manage the chaos? What you're talking about will create so much chaos that there is no *way* we can have any peace of mind!"

This question reveals a reasonable fear. If you constantly recalibrate and make continuous improvements every day, everywhere and with everyone, then how can you still provide stability?

The answer comes in what I call "organized chaos." We have to create broad parameters and practices that allow and encourage spontaneous change and perpetual innovation. When I think about organized chaos, I immediately think about my kids and my grandkids. Kids need room to play and boundaries to stay safe at the same time. Kids need only a few pieces of playground equipment for amusement and fences for safety, and they can create hours of seemingly random fun. Have you noticed that no one has to tell kids to play? They have a natural imagination and innovative spirit to make their own fun.

The practices and habits I've outlined in this book provide the tools, framework, and boundaries for "organized chaos" to flourish in your church. If you want all control, great! But recognize that you will never get growth, innovation, or progress.

Let me offer four exercises that will help you to create and cultivate managed chaos in your church. We manage every change initiative at New Life in one of these four chaotic buckets.

1. Three-minute conversations

It may shock you, but New Life makes changes all the time in three minutes or less. While this may sound reckless, most of the time it is not. In fact, I tend to waste too much time on decisions that deserve only three minutes of my emotional bandwidth.

In order to become a nimble and spontaneous organization, you need to acknowledge that many details and decisions deserve the least possible amount of your time. It's easy for leaders to waste emotional energy on details and decisions that simply don't merit more than a few moments. Far too often, church leaders seem to take three decades to make progress in an area that should take only three minutes. An exaggeration? Maybe, but not by much.

Many leaders come to New Life to view our weekend gatherings. One of the most common comments we receive is, "I'm surprised at how you often make changes on the spot." They watch us coach teaching pastors, host pastors, change service orders, encourage a volunteer, and so much more. It often shocks them how quickly we make continuous improvements. But once kaizen becomes a cultural operating system, it becomes the normal way of doing business.

Three-minute conversations require leaders to develop their leadership intuition. They need to learn to follow their intuition or, as my wife likes to say, "Go with your gut." Don't be afraid to make a continuous improvement on the spot. If your gut tells you, "This is not the right direction," go with it. I am not suggesting irresponsible decision-making, but am insisting that leaders need to make continuous improvements all the time.

This is particularly true on Sundays. If something is happening in your service that doesn't resonate with you or does make you cringe, don't worry overmuch about people's feelings; change on demand. Fix the service order, get rid of the boring announcement video, change a song, drop an illustration or joke in the message that's not working. If you are willing to make your own continual improvements, others will more easily accept your suggestions for them. (Warning: Some of these things may be load-bearing walls and you can't do load-bearing changes in three minutes.)

> If something is happening in your service that doesn't resonate with you or does make you cringe, don't worry overmuch about people's feelings; change on demand.

Making continuous improvements during a weekend gathering at New Life is such a cultural norm that we have established a new rule of thumb: bring up only the continuous improvements that can be made on the spot. Anything else can wait. We don't always obey this rule, but it helps us manage our conversations and expectations.

2. Three-day improvements

Some things that we know aren't working need to be changed within three days. Many times, this includes something associated with Sunday's gathering, but it can relate to any ministry or system.

Remember that every Sunday is just 165 hours away from the last one. In church life, we have to learn how to make continuous improvements within three days, or the church will become dry and sluggish almost overnight.

I have met many leaders who suffer the same cringe moment Sunday after Sunday, even though many of these issues can be fixed in three days or less. For some reason, however, we don't pull the trigger. I know leaders who have the same usher bothering them week after week, month after month, decade after decade. Why? If you are unwilling to deal with this problem...you deserve the problem.

We discuss three-day improvements in staff meetings, service programming meetings (where we review weekend services), over email, one-on-one, in the restroom, and on the fly. We are not afraid to say, "Fix this by Sunday."

- If you have an ugly sign in the restroom, don't look at it week after week. Take it down. Don't ask a committee to decide this issue. Solve it in three days.
- If one of your staff members has an attitude problem, talk to him or her. Don't let the issue fester.
- If a musician is unreliable, address the issue before the next Sunday.
- If the nursery equipment needs cleaning, get it cleaned.

3. Three-month initiatives

This is the most powerful way New Life manages chaos. If something can't be solved in three minutes or three days, typically it takes no more than three months. (By the way, this may be one indication it may be a load-bearing wall.) It may take a bit less than that or a bit more—maybe two months or five—but it doesn't have to take anywhere close to a year.

New Life typically does two three-month initiatives each year. One occurs in the fall (late September or early October) and one in the spring (mid-February or early March). Additionally, other three-month initiatives are happening all the time within various departments.

The three-month initiative in the spring tends to focus on relaunching something that impacts the entire church (adding a service, adding a campus, etc.), while the one in the fall tends to focus on departments and leadership structure. Consider a few three-month initiatives that New Life has tackled over the years:

Small groups. We have recalibrated our small group strategy four times in the last twelve years. We went from a Sunday school model to a closed group model. We went from closed group model to an open group model. We went from an open group model to a message-based model.

We recently recalibrated our discipleship model. Our approach transformed from an overly organized, restrictive process to a grassroots movement featuring simple study guides and videos.

Assimilation. The staff, elders, and other influencers took ninety days to focus on assimilation. We read key books on the subject, called other churches to find out what they were doing, reviewed all the letters and emails we send out to first and second-time guests, and more. As a result, today we have a great assimilation process, because we had the discipline to focus long enough to get the desired results.

Water baptism. This was one of the most significant initiatives we ever adopted. For three months at every staff meeting, we included time to discuss how to create a culture of water baptism. We involved the elders, talked to other churches, brainstormed, studied Scripture, and created a language around water baptism appropriate to our church. We spent ninety days focusing on how to create a culture that reflects the importance of water baptism.

Stewardship. We spent three months recalibrating the stewardship culture at New Life. During this same time, we read, asked questions, and reviewed all of the best practices for creating a culture of generosity and stewardship. As a result, over the last twelve years, our giving has increased 7 to 10 percent annually.

My preaching. This is a personal ninety-day recalibration initiative. Over the last twelve years, I have recalibrated my preaching three times. During each initiative, I asked questions, listened to myself preach, read books, and prayed for wisdom and insight. Many churches are stuck and ingrown because the pastor is still locked into a preaching style appropriate for the church's needs of two decades ago. It got embedded into the culture back then and continues to hang on today.

4. Three-year cultural recalibration

The foundation of this book is built on this single premise. Some seismic and cultural issues can't be solved in three minutes, three days, or even three months. They require a cultural recalibration.

As I've said, you need a cultural, holistic recalibration every three to five years.

It's almost shocking how closely New Life has kept to this cycle in the last ninety years. For my doctoral program, you may recall that I read all the board minutes from 1928 to 2003. Every time the church recalibrated, it kept on mission; when it didn't, the church stagnated and drifted off mission.

The Story of Canvas Church

I have worked for years with a great leader named Kevin Geer. For four of those years, Kevin served on my teaching team. During that time, he learned how to develop a culture of recalibration.

In August 2012, Kevin became the lead pastor of an established church in Montana. His church, Christian Center, has a rich history spanning eighty-nine years.

Before Kevin arrived, the church had an interim pastor for fifteen months. When Kevin became the pastor, he found no clear leadership at the top. Many in the church and on staff felt discouraged by dwindling attendance and decreasing financial giving. Every department had a silo mentality and an attitude to match. The culture was inwardly focused, basically just trying to survive. The pastoral team did not know how to collaborate and had no relational connection to each other. Small decisions got mired in discussions heading nowhere, leading to a "hunker down and survive" mentality. The most influential voices in the church seemed to be hyper-spiritual prayer warrior/prophet types.

Because Kevin understands the principles and practices of recalibration, during his first year, he leveraged his "honeymoon period" to create a new culture of recalibration. He immediately began to rethink everything about Christian Center. He also knew he had to skillfully deal with some load-bearing walls and carefully realign the culture of the church.

Deep inside his heart, Kevin knew God wanted to do something fresh at Christian Center. And so he confronted the status quo. He walked the church through a Rethink Phase.

Practically, this meant:

- Staff realignment and layoffs
- Office moves and new hires
- A new style of worship
- Stage attire, auditory volume, physical environment, and lighting were no longer up for endless discussion

Kevin spent a lot of time realigning the culture of the church. Realigning the vision and direction of the congregation resulted in a significant shift of lay people who had wielded power and influence. Either the "old guard" found themselves disenfranchised, or they jumped on board. He created a new cultural lexicon, celebrated short-terms wins, and cast a clear vision to the church.

In the fall of 2014, Kevin knew the time had come to relaunch Christian Center. He created a time-bound, well-defined, mission-critical Relaunch Initiative. He set the date. He defined the changes. He acted.

The Relaunch Initiative recalibrated Christian Center. It became a new church, complete with a new name: Canvas Church. The church started a new building update, created a new vision, and defined a new direction.

This new name offered the church a great opportunity to re-introduce itself to the community. "Canvas Church" clearly said, "This is definitely not your grandfather's church!" The mission of Canvas Church is "creating opportunities to experience God in a life-changing way."

As a result of this Relaunch Initiative, Canvas has seen increases in attendance, conversions, baptisms, giving, and serving. Kevin understands the leadership practice of continuous improvements. Already he has led his church through several of them:

- Fall of 2013: Canvas started Softer Sundays, featuring a different worship style to reach a crowd that prefers that type of music.
- Fall of 2014: Canvas added a Saturday evening gathering, a Spanish language gathering, and online gatherings during main weekend services.
- Easter of 2015: Canvas added a campus in East Glacier, Montana.
- Fall of 2015: The church kicked off Canvas Connect, with Life Groups, Activity Groups, and Canvas University groups.

As growth continues, Canvas is now in discussions about when to add a third Sunday morning gathering. The members are asking probing and piercing questions about how to become more a part of the fabric of their community as they seek to make Jesus famous in Montana's Flathead Valley.

A Prophetic Word for You

I tell this story about Kevin and Canvas Church because I believe God wants to recalibrate your church!

With all my heart, I believe the best days of your church and ministry are in front of you, not behind you. As I write, I see this as a prophetic word for thousands of pastors and leaders across North America. God has not given up on His bride! Nor has God given up on your church. He is looking for leaders who have the courage and confidence to lead their churches into a better future. He has placed you in this church at this time to lead its renewal through a recalibration of its mission. He has given you the gifts and the resources to accomplish this mission.

The spiritual giants of your church have sacrificed so much in the past! The best way to honor their sacrifice is to recalibrate *your* church for an even brighter future.

Coaching Assignments

1. How can you encourage a mindset of continuous improvement among your staff? Among your board members? Your influencers? Your core leaders? Your volunteers?

2. Where do you feel tempted to go for perfection when you need to strive for improvement? How has this perfectionist mindset hampered the growth of your church? How can you change it?

3. Consider how you can create a culture of continuous improvements:

    *   Three-minute conversations: What three-minute conversations do you need to have this week? What can they change in your church?

    *   Three-day improvements: What three-day improvements will help move your church forward? Describe them.

    *   Three-month initiatives: What three-month initiatives do you need to consider now or in the future? What department or leadership issues need this kind of sustained focus?

    *   Three-year cultural recalibration: Does your church need a cultural recalibration? What is God birthing in your heart? How can your church reach its full Kingdom impact?

Part Five

THE FINAL CHALLENGE

Just a few years ago, I was standing one Sunday in the back of the church, getting ready to preach. As I looked at the congregation, I heard the still, small voice of God say to me, "Take care of your own soul, and I will take care of My church." This personal, intimate whisper from God reminded me that I am a follower of Jesus first and a leader second.

Recognize, leader, that the hardest person in your church to lead and recalibrate is the one staring back at you in the mirror. That means that recalibrating your church is really all about recalibrating *you!*

Whenever I teach this recalibrate material in any kind of setting, I can almost see the audience getting ready to ask me several kinds of questions:

- How does a leader keep healthy in middle of the ups and downs of life?
- How does a leader keep his heart and soul right in the middle of all the changes of our culture?
- How does a leader take care of her own spiritual life and soul?
- How does a leader sleep at night?

While this is not a book on spiritual transformation, I care too deeply about you not to spend at least a few moments on the subject. And I must insist that if you recalibrate your church, but don't take care of your own soul . . . at the end of the day, it really won't matter. If you neglect to take care of your soul, everything you just read is worthless.

This is by far the most important part of the book.

14

RECALIBRATE YOUR SOUL

About forty-eight months into my leadership at New Life, I knew something had gone terribly wrong with the condition of my soul. While the church was gaining some traction and I looked fine on the outside, on the inside I was slowing dying.

The personal turbulences, hurts, and disappointments I had navigated in order to lead the church to a better place had taken a real toll on me. The misfires, setbacks, and departing people were slowly eating away at my soul, one day at a time. They were building barriers between me and my staff and rotting away my inner strength.

During this dark time, I decided to see a counselor. At our very first session, I began our time by saying, "*Pastor* Troy is doing fine, but *Follower of Jesus* Troy is struggling."

I soon found that I needed to recalibrate more than my leadership of the church; I needed to recalibrate my own soul. I needed to recalibrate my passion for God and His presence in my life.

You've already seen that I believe passionately in the local church. For that reason, I believe pastors need to boldly lead their churches into a culture of recalibration. But let me very clear: God cares far more about your love for Him than about your work for Him.

And that means the greatest thing you need to recalibrate is your spiritual health. If you can't take care of yourself, then nothing else really matters. Christ Himself reminded us, "For what does it profit a man to gain the whole world and forfeit his soul?" (Mark 8:36).

Renovation of the Heart

In his insightful book *Renovation of the Heart*, Dallas Willard speaks candidly about what truly goes on inside all of us: "The part of us that drives and organizes our life is not the physical. You have a spirit within you and it has been formed. It has taken on a specific character."[90] He adds, "Our life and how we find the world now and in the future is, almost totally, a simple result of what we have become in the depths of our being—in our spirit, will, or heart."[91]

I love how Willard describes the process of spiritual formation as a renovation of the heart: "Accordingly, the greatest need you and I have—the greatest need of collective humanity—is renovation of our heart. That spiritual place within us from which outlook, choices, and actions come has been formed by a world away from God. Now it must be transformed."[92]

I echo his stirring declaration. The greatest need of collective humanity—and of each one of us—is a personal recalibration of the soul. The alternative is unthinkable.

Deceptively Healthy Leaders

In chapter 2, I discussed how a church can become "deceptively healthy." This is true not only of churches, but of pastors and leaders, too. I would even push it further and say that one of the main reasons churches become deceptively healthy is that their leaders become deceptively healthy.

As a Christian leader, it is very easy to fall into this trap of deceptive spiritual health. Everything looks good on the inside, but deep inside, you are rotting away. You have grown spiritually dry.

Something is wrong and you know it . . . but you ignore it. It is easy to preach the Word, pray public prayers, and minister to people, while at the same time drifting farther and farther from God.

And yet you are not in full rebellion. It is actually far more subtle than that. You are in full denial of the deteriorated condition of your soul.

In my doctoral studies, I had a class with Dr. Roger Heuser, professor of leadership studies at Vanguard University, called "Spiritual Formation and Soul Care of Others." At first, I thought this class would prove useless for a bunch of preachers. I entertained decidedly cynical thoughts about it: *Leaders, especially at this point of their education, don't need this!*

I was wrong. The truth is that church leaders can fall into the trap of being deceptively healthy more easily and more often than Christian leaders in the marketplace. It is very easy to become a professional Christian when you are in professional ministry.

> **The truth is that church leaders can fall into the trap of being deceptively healthy more easily and more often than Christian leaders in the marketplace.**

This class introduced me to the work of M. Robert Mulholland, Jr. Mulholland wrote a number of books that warn of what he calls the "false self." We take on this false self "when we are dependent on our own strength and trusting in our human resources and abilities and not a radical trust in God."[93]

He discusses the extreme subtlety of the false self, especially for church leaders: "The false self is so subtle in the ways it sinks its roots into things other than God, especially when you are engaged in God's work."[94] The last part of this quote particularly caught my attention: *especially when you are engaged in God's work.*

This is so true! When you are engaged in ministry, it is breathtakingly easy to lose your personal and intimate relationship with God and not even know it. God created us to depend totally on Him, not on our own strengths and abilities. Mulholland says you were created to experience your ultimate value "in an intimate, loving union with God at the core of your being."[95]

Some of us need a spiritual awakening! We need to recalibrate our souls. We need a fresh, bracing encounter with the living God. We need an intimate, loving union with God at the core of our being. Don't lose sight of the radical truth: God cares far more about you than He does about your ministry.

Mulholland digs even deeper into this deceptively healthy state by discussing a "religious false self" that is even more difficult for us to identify and acknowledge. He discusses how easy it is to camouflage our religious false self: "Our religious false self may be rigorous in religiosity, devoted in discipleship and sacrificial in service—without being in loving union with God."[96] In other words, we do all the right things, but we have drifted from our first love.

Our religious false self is the greatest enemy of Christian leaders. It also presents the most deadly trap before us. Why? Because it is so very easy.

It is very easy to become a professional Christian and lose your passion for God.

It is very easy, over time, to let your soul get embittered.

It is easy to stop paying attention to your love and passion for Jesus.

It is easy to put your Christianity on autopilot.

We so easily fool ourselves. We are deceptively healthy, and we don't even know it. The soul dies while everything on the outside appears just fine.

Mulholland argues that "successful" church programs and events can give us a false sense of security: "A welter of worship services,

Bible studies, prayer meetings, accountability groups, fellowship meetings, retreats and workshops often enable us to calm our fears and assure ourselves that our religious identity and value is secure."[97] He describes how the accolades of our fans only reinforce this religious false self: "Of course, the praise and adulation we usually receive for all these activities further serve to confirm the validity of our idol and the box in which it is kept."[98]

How Is Your Soul Doing?

The soul is your inner being, your inmost existence. The soul is everything within you. Your soul is who you are, while the body is just a temporary shell. Your body is simply a container for your spirit.

Genesis 2:7 records the creation of the first man: "Then the LORD God formed a man from the dust of the ground and breathed into his nostrils the breath of life, and the man became a living being." God formed you and then breathed into your nostrils the breath of life, *His* life. The body is just a lifeless shell. It is the breath of God that gives you life. Every breath we take is a gift from God!

We need God to breathe into our nostrils the breath of life. We all need to fall flat on our faces and hear from God. While you need to get a divine assignment for your church, your deeper and continual need is to get a divine breath for your life.

Recalibrating your soul requires you to get brutally honest about your soul and what is going on deep inside of you. It requires you to look deep down at your religious false self and ask deep questions about the condition of your soul. So let me ask:

How is your soul doing?

I know this may seem like a strange question. It feels a bit personal, maybe overly so. Very few people will ever ask you such a personal question. And yet, I need to ask it: How is your soul doing?

The question may seem as strange as if someone were to walk into my house and ask, "How is your home's foundation?" If you were to walk into my house, you might make all kinds of comments about the décor and other outward trappings; nothing wrong with that. But none of these things keep my house standing. If the foundation has a big crack or has begun rotting away, I will be in trouble. No one has ever said to me, "Troy, your foundation is awesome!" Nor has anyone ever asked, "May I look at your foundation?" It just doesn't happen. Most people never see my house's foundation, nor would they have any reason to do so.

How is your soul doing?

All of us tend to focus on the outward stuff. If our floors look good and the house looks great, what's the problem? But the real issue, ultimately, is the foundation. Unfortunately, the only time someone wants to see my home's foundation is when erosion occurs or a crack appears. Otherwise, no one pays any attention.

The same is true in church leadership. We seldom ask questions about foundational issues unless someone falls morally, has a breakdown, or just checks out of the game. So let me be the one to pry into your life and ask you a probing and piercing question: How is your soul doing?

How is the foundation of your life?

Do you passionately love God?

Are you trapped in your religious false self?

Do you have all the symptoms of being deceptively healthy?

At the core of your being, *how is your soul doing?*

Why Recalibrate the Soul?

I want to be very clear here. The reason we church leaders need to recalibrate our souls is not so that we can be better leaders, but so we can have an intimate union and total dependency on God. We need total reliance on God, not on ourselves. You don't recalibrate your soul so you can preach better, lead better, or in some way grow your church. You recalibrate your soul so you can love God and walk in union with Him.

A great book by author and pastor Wayne Cordeiro has had an incredible influence on my life. In *Leading on Empty: Refilling Your Tank and Renewing Your Passion*, he recounts his own personal journey of living on adrenaline while dying on the inside and leading on empty. He describes his emotional state at this dark moment: "My vision for the church was barren, and the once-alive heart that beat incessantly for others had begun to shrink."[99] He says something so essential to all those who desire to recalibrate their churches: "It is a gift to be able to launch an inspiring vision. But unless you manage it along the way, it can turn on you, and soon the voracious appetite of the vision consumes you.[100]

Unless you manage your vision along the way, it will kill both you and your soul. It's easy to be more consumed with your vision than the God who gave it to you. The warning God gave to the church in Ephesus is a prophetic word for leaders and pastors: "Consider how far you have fallen! Repent and do the things you did at first. If you do not repent, I will come to you and remove your lampstand from its place" (Revelation 2: 5–6).

God is calling His church and leaders back to their first love, but not so they can become a better leader or minister or grow the church. God is calling you back to your first love because He wants you to love Him.

At the end of the day, this is all that matters.

How to Recalibrate Your S.O.U.L.

Cordeiro gives leaders a clear warning: "The only way to finish strong will be to first replenish your system. If you don't, prepare for a crash."[101] You cannot finish strong if you don't replenish or recalibrate your own soul! You will crash.

I'd like to offer four guiding principles and practices to recalibrate and replenish the soul (abbreviated by S.O.U.L. = Search, Obey, Unplug, Let go). This isn't some kind of checklist you do every day to feel better. But so often we do approach spiritual transformation like a checklist:

- ✔ I read my Bible today.
- ✔ I prayed today.
- ✔ I was nice to my spouse.
- ✔ I did all the right things.
- ✔ I didn't do any wrong things.

Each of us has to get away from the skewed mentality that behavior and effort alone will change us. The four actions of S.O.U.L. (Search, Obey, Unplug, Let go) must be infused into the very fabric of your life. At some level, I live out these behaviors in every conversation, every decision I make, every night before I go to bed. I have ingrained them into the fabric of my life. You must take these principles designed to help you recalibrate your soul very seriously.

Search your heart

As Willard so carefully reminds us, spiritual formation is a renovation of the heart. Followers of Jesus Christ must honestly search their hearts. The only way to combat becoming a deceptively healthy person and putting on your religious false self is to humble yourself before God and daily search your heart in His presence.

David prayed, "Search me, God, and know my heart; test me and know my anxious thoughts. See if there is any offensive way in me, and lead me in the way everlasting" (Psalm 139: 23-24). Pray this prayer with King David every day! God is the only one who truly can search your heart.

One of my life's Scriptures is Proverbs 4:18: "Above all else, guard your heart, for it is the wellspring of life." This Scripture is at the core of my spiritual formation. Above everything we do, we must guard our hearts. This is the very core of what happens in my life. It doesn't matter how much I pray, fast, read Scripture, or claim spiritual transformation; I have to guard my heart from the poison of the day.

Everything comes from the heart. If people change their actions but never deal with the heart, then they have missed the whole concept of spiritual formation. So every day I try to ask this question: "How is my heart?"

We live in a culture where everything is about image. We live with this "tyranny of the image." As a result, we start fooling ourselves.

How many "likes" did I get on a comment I posted on Facebook? How many Twitter followers do I have? How many pictures can I post on Instagram to give the impression that everything is okay in my life? It's not hard to fool your followers on social media. You may even be able to fool yourself. But God looks at the inside, at your heart.

> **God speaks to us every day, deep within our souls.**

So really, what is going on inside? Do you hold any offenses or grudges against anyone? Are you seeking God? How is your heart doing? Is it full of God? Or is it full of bitterness and the sinful stuff of this life?

Obey the still, small voice of God

I like the language of "the still, small voice" of God, taken from an account about the prophet Elijah in 1 Kings. The discouraged prophet had asked God to speak to him, and in reply Elijah heard loud noise and saw impressive fury—but he got no message from God. Only in a still, quiet moment did Elijah hear his Creator's voice.

God has never spoken to me in an audible way, but I can say He often speaks to me in the still, small voice. When someone whispers to you, it communicates intimacy and personal connection. It's exclusive. It signifies importance. When someone whispers to you, it means that he or she has something special and specific for you, meant for no one else. When my wife whispers in my ear, "I love you," it is very personal.

God speaks to us every day, deep within our souls. I did not write this book to get into the difference between discernment, intuition, and gut feelings, but I do believe God uses all these ways to speak to us. Learn to pause and listen to His still, small voice, whether you're a pastor, a business leader, a ministry coordinator, or anyone else who belongs to Him. God wants to be personal with you. God wants to speak to you, in a whisper.

If we listen to God's still, small voice, it will protect us and help us to navigate the fierce winds of change that threaten to blow us over. That voice:

- Protects us from temptation
- Teaches us personal character and holiness
- Guides our decision making
- Instructs us on wise timing
- Provides us with providential direction for our churches

As followers of Jesus, we need to learn to listen to and obey the still, small voice of God.

Unplug from noise and chaos

The primary enemy preventing us from hearing the still, small voice of God is noise and chaos. A noisy room makes it hard to hear someone's whisper. And yet, our world, our churches, and our lives are chock full of noise.

The TV is always on in our homes. The radio is blaring in the car. Text alerts continually beep at us. Social media status updates keep us perpetually distracted. Noise, noise, noise! Noise will kill your soul.

Study the life of Jesus. Mark's Gospel tells us how Jesus was able to unplug from the noise and chaos: "Very early in the morning, while it was still dark, Jesus got up, left the house and went off to a solitary place, where he prayed" (Mark 1:35).

Many of us can't pray because we don't know how to unplug from the noise and chaos of the day. We continually check our email, respond to a text, or look at our social media. When did you last spend some time in solitude, quieting your heart, eliminating all distractions and allowing yourself adequate time just to listen to God? I know I'm getting very personal here, but it's a crucial question. If your spiritual life feels as dry as kindling, then you need to recalibrate your soul.

> **Many of us can't pray because we don't know how to unplug from the noise and chaos of the day.**

Hearing God's still, small voice requires us to pause long enough to unplug from the noise and chaos of the day . . . and just *listen*. For years, I have followed a simple model suggested by Rick Warren. Here it is:

Divert daily: I find times every day to search my heart, obey the still, small voice of God, and unplug from noise and chaos. I take time in the morning and before I go to bed to journal, read Scripture, and listen to God speak to me.

Withdraw weekly: We all need a Sabbath. Especially preachers. I consider my day off (Friday) as my Sabbath. I honor this day. My wife and I have a date night most Friday nights. I have been dating her for twenty-six years! We have three or four evenings home every week.

Abandon annually: I take vacations. Twice a year, I have a personal prayer and planning retreat. I have done twenty-seven of these since 1997. My wife Jana and I just finished a Sabbatical last year.

A bit of warning here. In regard to soul care, we need to respect the fact that everyone is unique. Over the years, my wife and I have struggled with learning to respect each other's approaches to recalibrating the soul. Soul care and spiritual transformation looks different for all of us. My wife and I do not approach spiritual growth in the same way. While we both care deeply about having a healthy soul, we differ in how we recalibrate the soul.

- She is a morning person; I am a night owl.
- I journal in bullet points what God speaks to me; she prays and listens to God.
- I hear God speak in the hot tub; she hears God speak when she is alone.
- When she prays, demons shudder; when I pray . . . trust me, it's not like her praying.
- I go to a restaurant to read my Bible; she sits behind a piano and reflects deeply.
- She has three Bible reading plans; I have one Bible reading plan.
- She reads ahead of her Bible reading plan; I use the "catch me up" button on YouVersion.

Respect how each individual unplugs from noise and chaos and recalibrates the soul!

Let go of things that poison the soul

Hurt and bitterness rot the soul of a leader more than anything else. Have people hurt you? Certainly. But your response to those offenses, hurts, and disappointments is what will make or break you—you have to let them go.

I have met so many leaders full of poison. Their last church didn't treat them right. The board members are idiots. People have let them down. The staff doesn't support them. Leaders can harbor all types of grievances deep down in their souls.

I am not a counselor. I understand that sometimes this issue of harboring bitterness takes counseling beyond a book. I have personally benefited from counseling, big time. But at the end of the day, you have to let go of all the hurt and pain inside of you.

Let it go every day. Every day before I go to bed, I forgive those who hurt me. I make sure my soul is good. I can't say this is easy! At times, it takes longer than a day.

A very disappointing event just happened in my life, and I started venting about it to my wife. She looked at me and said, "You have forty-eight hours to vent and throw up all you want. But after this, let it go!" Not a bad piece of wisdom.

So many things eat at the soul:

- Bitterness
- Disappointment
- Failure
- People
- Loneliness
- Insecurity

You must guard your soul against offenses, hurts and bitterness. Forgive quickly. Unforgiveness is like a cancer that rots and eats away the best part of you. It clouds your vision and your love for people. The single greatest emotional danger you face is bitterness toward those who have hurt and disappointed you.

What My Niece Taught Me on Her Deathbed

I can't think of a better way to close this chapter and this book than to talk about my niece, Kara Brown. At eighteen years of age, Kara was diagnosed with paroxysmal nocturnal hemoglobinuria (PNH), a rare blood disease.[102] It occurs when the protein layer that protects red blood cells becomes compromised, and the immune system begins to damage those cells. It is extremely rare and life threatening.

Kara had two bone marrow transplants in a just a few years. She went through chemo, blood transfusions, and many surgeries, then developed diabetes from all her medications, lost all her hair, spent months at Seattle Children's Hospital, and lived in the Pete Gross House complex for transplant patients, next to the Seattle Cancer Care Alliance. From the bone marrow transplants, she developed a disease called graft-versus-host disease (GVHD).

> "Don't hold on to the crap of life. All the hurt is not important. Don't hold on to it. People really do care—they just don't know how to show it. You need to give people room to grow."

The GVHD ate her from the inside out. She couldn't eat food. Her digestive system was shutting down and no one could do anything about it. Her parents, doctors, and family members attempted everything to save her life.

Kara's final wish in 2010 was to spend Thanksgiving with her family. She came home and the entire family gathered. She arrived in an ambulance. (And by the way, in a special gift from her Creator, it snowed that day. Kara loved the snow.)

We all knew she only had days with us. Everyone in the family said their final goodbyes. I had a few moments alone with Kara. I knew this would be the last time we talked. Her parents already had asked me to do her memorial. I wanted her legacy to be shared and known. As I sat in her room, I could feel the presence of God.

I asked Kara, "How do you want your life to be celebrated? What is your story that you want to be told?" I listened carefully and took notes. I wanted to make sure I did my best for her.

She looked at me and said very softly, "The only day you will ever regret is the day of not serving Jesus. I wish I could have given Him more. I so love Him." Then she started crying. It was a profound moment.

But clearly, Kara had more she wanted to say. After a moment, she looked up and with a very weak voice—almost like the still, small voice of God—she said, "Don't hold on to the crap of life. All the hurt is not important. Don't hold on to it. People really do care—they just don't know how to show it. You need to give people room to grow."

What a way to finish my book! I tell this story for many reasons. First, heed the wisdom of my niece: "Don't hold onto the crap of life." Leaders tend to do exactly that. Don't!

Second, it puts everything into perspective for me. You *will* face turbulence and disappointments. People *will* let you down. People *will* say all types of unfair things about you, especially behind your back. Let the words of my niece encourage you: "People really do care—they just don't know how to show it."

I've written this book to help you recalibrate your church, but make sure you take care of your own soul! Never forget that God cares more about your soul than He does about all your church work.[103]

Coaching Assignments

1. Find some trusted friends and discuss with them the question, "How is your soul doing?" This is a tough question, but one that will determine your entire life.

2. Walk through the four practices of soul care. How can you daily learn to:

   • Search your heart?

   • Obey the still, small voice of God?

   • Unplug from noise?

   • Let go of bitterness?

3. What practical rhythms can you establish in your life to keep your soul healthy? Daily rhythms? Weekly rhythms? Annual rhythms?

APPENDIX A

RECALIBRATION FOUND IN SCRIPTURE AND CHURCH HISTORY

Creation of Heaven and Earth (Genesis 1–2)

When God created the heavens and the earth, He calibrated the world. He set in motion the order of the universe and the laws that govern the natural world. He made man in His own image, blessing humanity and issuing what I call the first commission: "Be fruitful and increase in number; fill the earth and subdue it'" (Genesis 1:28). This idyllic, perfect reality expresses the default settings for man's relationship to both creation and Creator.

The Garden (Genesis 3)

When Adam and Eve sinned, they threw all relationships, both natural and divine, into chaos. God then recalibrated the trajectory of all humanity by offering redemption to His fallen children. God promised that He would set humanity back on course, using Adam and Eve. He set the basic rules for a recalibrated reality: God covers sin; sacrifice atones for failure; man cannot redeem himself, but needs forgiveness from God.

The Flood (Genesis 5–9)

Man's corruption and sin reached the point where God regretted creating humanity. God literally recalibrated humanity by destroying the earth through a worldwide flood. Afterwards, God established a covenant with humanity in which He promised He would never again destroy created life. He returned humanity to the first commission, saying to Noah and his three sons, "Be fruitful and increase in number and fill the earth."

The Tower of Babel (Genesis 11)

The people wanted to settle down and build a tower, apparently hoping to become like God and reach Him on their own terms. Their efforts represented a defiance of God's plan for redemption and demonstrated the temptation toward self-reliance. God confused their language and recalibrated the people by forcing them to disperse all over the earth. As a result of this recalibration, humanity is scattered "over the face of the whole earth."

The Patriarchs (Genesis 12–50)

After God's recalibration of humanity at the tower of Babel, the human race continued to spiral downward in selfishness, pride, and despair. As a result, God created a new covenant with humankind, making an elderly and childless couple the launch pad of His whole mission of redemption. God used Abraham, Isaac, Jacob, and Joseph as the early patriarchs to recalibrate humanity and ultimately form the nation of Israel.

The Promised Land (Exodus–Joshua)

After four hundred years of Egyptian oppression, Israel had lost its sacred identity. Through Moses, God recalibrated His people and reminded them of their place in His plan and their destiny to be a light of God's grace to the nations. By giving God's law to a lost and conquered people, Moses returned Israel to its true identity.

Because of the Israelites' stubbornness and continual complaining, and because of Moses' disobedience, God established new leadership. Everyone who had left Egypt, except for Caleb and Joshua, died outside of the Promised Land. God recalibrated his people once again under the leadership of Joshua, who led them into Canaan and commanded their march to claim their sacred homeland (and reclaim God's promises).

Judges and Kings

For three hundred years, Israel had no king. Instead, God appointed judges to lead His people. These judges were holy men (and one woman), all of them called by God. They led the Israelites in battle and delivered them from foreign oppressors. They helped the people to serve God. And after their leadership successes, they modeled true servant leadership by returning to their homes and fields, often openly rejecting praise or the opportunity to rule.

As Israel transitioned to a monarchy, God gave the nation Saul, who failed as a leader and reminded Israel of her need for righteousness. Through Samuel, God appointed David to be king, creating the ideal ruler for Israel and a prototype of the rule of Christ.

Poets and Prophets

God raised up poets and prophets to recalibrate the people's passion and love for Him. Isaiah spoke of a Suffering Servant who would redeem God's people from their sin (Isaiah 53). Jeremiah envisioned a time when the law would not be written on stone, but rather on the hearts of humanity (Jeremiah 31). Malachi proclaimed that the Sun of Righteous would rise with healing in His wings (Malachi 4). Throughout these prophetic books, God consistently called His people to recalibrate their perspective and look forward to the coming Messiah.

The Life of Jesus

Jesus recalibrated humanity and the religious culture of the day. In His landmark Sermon on the Mount, Jesus recalibrated ethics, morality, and spirituality. By preaching to the

heart of issues, He took the commands of God off the books and placed them into hearts.

When Jesus died, He declared, "It is finished." Humanity could now have an unfettered relationship with God. In one sense, Jesus brought humanity back to the garden, where we can now approach God the Father with boldness and full assurance. The death, resurrection, and ascension of Christ recalibrated all humanity by bringing the eternal reality of direct access to God into everyday life, providing that free access to any and all who believe.

The Early Church (Acts)

Throughout the book of Acts, we see the church recalibrated again and again:

Acts 2. The Holy Spirit recalibrated the people of God and empowered them to take the gospel to Jerusalem, Judea, Samaria, and the uttermost parts of the earth.

Acts 6. God recalibrated the early church leadership. As the church grew, no longer could the ministry be contained to the twelve apostles. So they recalibrated and empowered others in the church to do ministry—and so the church grew again.

Acts 10. Peter himself faced a recalibration of huge significance. This is perhaps the most radical recalibration in Scripture: God speaks to Peter and shows him that the ethnic and cultural barriers to faith have been cast down. Gentiles now have unhindered access to the grace of God.

Acts 11 and 13. The church recalibrated because of the martyrdom of Stephen and the persecution of the early church. The church scattered throughout the region, a few of them taking the gospel to the Gentiles in Antioch. At this time, the followers of Jesus became a movement known as the "the way." At Antioch, the name of the movement got recalibrated to "Christians." New leadership emerged, especially through Barnabas and Saul. The church at Antioch sent out the church's first missionaries to the entire Roman Empire.

Acts 15. The church experienced a theological recalibration in what is perhaps the most critical recalibration moment for the first-century church. At the Jerusalem Council, Peter and James recalibrated the Jewish custom of circumcision. The Jerusalem Council's central issue focused on whether converted Gentiles could be truly redeemed if they remained uncircumcised and did not keep the Mosaic Law. Peter and James clearly recalibrated the church's view of soteriology and the role of grace in the life of all believers.

Paul the Apostle

God used Paul to help bring the gospel to the "uttermost parts of the world" (Acts 1:8). Paul recalibrated the church's view of Gentile mission and facilitated the spread of the gospel to the entire Gentile world.

Paul wrote thirteen of the twenty-seven books of the New Testament, and in his epistles, he repeatedly recalibrated the life of the church. Despite his pride in his Jewish heritage, Paul understood that redemption belongs to the Gentiles as well as to the Jews, so he traveled tirelessly throughout the ancient world, taking the message of salvation to the Gentiles.

Council of Nicaea, 325 A.D.

The Council of Nicaea recalibrated our understanding of Christ by defining a clear theology about the unique place of Jesus in the universe.

Protestant Reformation, 1517

Fueled by Martin Luther's personal journey of studying the book of Romans, which caused him to question the nature of European Christianity, the Reformation recalibrated our understanding of grace.

William Tyndale, 1525

Driven by a conviction that people should be able to read the Bible in their own language, Tyndale created the first English translation of the New Testament, thus recalibrating our access to Scripture.

Wesleyan Methodism, 1738

Rejecting a purely intellectual spirituality, John Wesley, through prayer and devotion, famously felt his "heart strangely warmed" and recalibrated our need for genuine spiritual experience.

Pentecostal Revival, 1901–1904

Inspired by a need to reach the world for Jesus Christ, church leaders sought the power of the Holy Spirit and recalibrated our empowerment for mission.

Creation of a New Heaven and Earth

One final day is coming when God will again recalibrate humanity. When He creates a new heaven and a new earth, every knee will bow at the name of Jesus.

APPENDIX B

RECALIBRATION FOR NEW LIFE CHURCH: 2003-2016

In the last ten years, New Life Church has undergone four major cultural recalibration moments. Let me briefly describe them for you.

December 2003: Becoming Lead Pastor

The catalyst for this first cultural recalibration was when I became lead pastor. In my first sermon series, "The House That God Built," I unplugged the church and then plugged it back in again. I used this honeymoon period to review and introduce a new cultural language. The series ended with a "Vision Night," where I cast a new vision that included reaching young families *and* honoring every generation throughout the process.

During my first couple of years as lead pastor, we:

- Recalibrated our mission, core values, and ministry model.
- Identified our mission-critical ministries as Sundays, children's ministry, and groups. We started to make changes accordingly in finances, staffing, resources, communication, and use of facilities.

- Recalibrated our worship culture. In three years, we went from orchestra and choir driven services to a contemporary style of worship.
- Recalibrated our target audience. We decided to target young families and focus on children's ministry, although we would continue to welcome all generations. Our vision to reach young families meant we needed all of the church's resources—staff, building, and volunteers—to be redirected toward children's ministries.
- Recalibrated our small group model. We have done this four times in the last twelve years.

One key way we recalibrated the culture of New Life was to start a new gathering called The Well, which met at 11:59AM as a third Sunday service. We never referred to it as a "contemporary service," nor did we market it as such. Still, I wanted to create an environment where I could experiment with how to approach church and let the new style slowly seep into the entire church. I wanted to feel good about the direction the church was going before I took everyone there. I told our staff, "We are *not* doing a contemporary service. We are doing a service that helps me discover the future of New Life."

I preached the first two services and then went into my office to change into jeans. I'd never preached in jeans as a lead pastor. It felt so strange. But The Well really did provide us with a live platform to rethink everything I'd ever thought about church. The Well gradually became the new culture at New Life.

Every time I got comfortable in my own skin, I began making gradual changes to the entire church. It amazed me to see that when I was authentic and looked comfortable, people tended to have an easier time following. For five years, we saw a good growth curve in The Well. After moving into our new building in the spring of 2010, all the services looked and felt like The Well. Eventually, we did away with The Well and made it our new normal.

Even though The Well caught on quickly and enjoyed immediate growth, I understood that we would lose an entire tribe of people if we didn't take other worship styles into consideration. So, six months later on August 15, 2004, we started Softer Sundays, a traditional style service featuring timeless music and hymns. Congregants heard and watched the sermon on a large video screen. Softer Sundays has grown over the years and continues to be part of our culture. It also served as a pilot program for our first video venue, allowing the congregation to see the message via video technology. Our current multi-site model features video preaching, but the pillars of the church were the first to accept and embrace the model.

2006: Recalibration Caused by Turmoil

Three years after I became the lead pastor, we faced another cultural recalibration. While the church was growing, we suffered some significant staff turnovers. People felt hurt, which broke my heart. I made stupid mistakes that I regret to this day. Frankly, my own lack of experience in leading and hiring staff hurt me.

To further complicate matters, a few core people at New Life chose this time to leave, which hurt me deeply. I still consider it one of the darkest, lowest periods of my life. It felt as though everyone wanted to jump ship at the same time.

I gained weight. I felt stressed. I plunged into emotional and spiritual bankruptcy. Candidly, the church was growing faster than me! I made mistakes and endured a series of events that caused me to wonder if I could survive. During this dark time, I had to recalibrate my own leadership and soul.

I thank God for a board that allowed me to invest in my professional growth and personal spiritual and emotional health. God used these unsettling moments of turmoil to recalibrate His church. During this period, we recalibrated the church in several shifts.

March 21, 2010: A New Building

Our new building, featuring a 1,600-seat auditorium, served as the catalyst for this recalibration. I knew that a building, by itself, wouldn't grow a church. We therefore treated this event as a massive cultural recalibration opportunity. We rebranded the church, updated the children's ministry, changed the service times, and rallied the church as if it were day one of the church's original planting. The results amazed all of us.

Overnight (or at least from Sunday, March 21 to Sunday, March 28, 2010) the church grew by 800 people! And we didn't stop growing after we moved into the new building. On January 16, 2011, just ten months after we started using the new auditorium, we began our first multi-site campus in the Maple Valley/Covington area. And on August 21, 2011, we baptized more than one hundred people in a single day, one of the biggest moments in our church's history.

2.12.12: Everything Changes

Two years after we moved into our new building, we underwent another cultural recalibration. Because of my doctoral study, I began asking, "What transferable principles can help churches to move forward?" That question caused me to examine another question I considered even more important: "Can we create the same energy to recalibrate the church, without a new pastor, a moral failure, or a new building?" We thought, *Why not?* And so we created a campaign called "Everything Changes, 2.12.12."

Operating as though we were planting a church for the first time, we purposefully created chaos. We announced to the church that we were starting over and that everyone should expect forty changes. We focused on a few key issues:

- We totally redid the children's ministry (again!).
- We rebranded our logo and website.

- We added a new Saturday night service.
- We changed the service times for Sunday morning to 9:30 and 11:15 AM.
- We officially started the phrase, "One church. Many campuses."
- We started a ten-chapter sermon series called the "The Jesus Story," which lasted two full years.

2.12.12 became a catalytic moment for New Life. About 1,100 people showed up for our inaugural Saturday night service—a new cultural beginning for us as a church family.

3.16.16: I See A Church

As I finished the final chapters of this book, New Life was in the middle of our fifth cultural recalibration. This time, we called all the campuses together for a vision night on Wednesday, March 16, 2016. We truly had unbelievable energy in the house when more than 1,800 people showed up to hear the new vision of New Life and what God was speaking to us for our next chapter.

We launched eight new initiatives:

1. *The largest care initiative in the history of New Life.*

   We are empowering 100 deacons to care for:

   - Widows/elderly people
   - Orphans/fatherless children
   - Hurting families and marriages
   - New Lifers in moments of crisis
   - First responders throughout our communities.

2. *A movement that challenges men to step up and leave a godly legacy.*

   The initial gathering will be June 8, 2016.

3. *A culture that encourages everyone to develop a life of prayer and personal devotion to Scripture.*

   We provided everyone with a SOAP journal.

4. *Three hundred sixteen serve projects in our community in thirty days.*

   These were scheduled from March 16-April 16.

5. *Identify and empower 100 emerging ministry leaders.*

6. *Add new campuses in Kent and Bellevue.*

   By 2020, New Life will be "One Church…Five Campuses."

7. *Pay off our existing mortgage.*

   We plan to do this by 2025.

8. *Officially launch a new ministry called "Kingdom Builders."*

   This includes men and women who are committed to use their finances to build the Kingdom of God in the Pacific Northwest and the world.

APPENDIX C

ııılııılııılııılııılııılııılııılııılııılıı

PROBING AND PIERCING QUESTIONS

From Larry Osborne: "Zero-Basing" Questions[1]

At North Coast Church, one of the most powerful tools we've used to help us keep our eyes on the target and regularly make the adjustments needed has been a process called "zero-basing." A zero-based meeting or retreat gathers a small group of key leaders and simply asks:

- What would we do differently if we were starting all over?
- If there were no backlash to worry about, what would we drop?
- What would we start?
- What would we change?
- How does the reality of our ministry match with our stated vision and goals?
- What would we do differently if our only boundary was a radical commitment to the Great Commission?

From Larry Osborne: Innovation Questions[2]

To identify the programs, processes, and policies that are most ripe for innovation and change, step back and ask yourself, "What frustrates me most?"

- What is it that drives me crazy?
- What are we doing that makes absolutely no sense?
- What processes and programs seem to take lots of work, but bear no fruit?
- What traditions are we putting up with simply because it has always been done this way?
- What is the one problem that if we could solve it, most of our other problems would go away?
- What's broken that seems to be unfixable?
- What problems are we living with because everyone says, "That's just the way it is"?

From Craig Groeschel: Questions to Stir Vision[3]

- Why does your organization exist? (If you can't answer this clearly, I'll bet you an overpriced latte that there are a few things your organization should stop doing immediately.)
- What can your organization be the best in the world at? (Borrowing from Jim Collins in *Good to Great*.)
- If you could do only one thing, what would it be?
- If you left your organization tomorrow, what would you hope would continue forever?
- What breaks your heart, keeps you awake at night, wrecks you?

From Bill Hybels: Questions to Clarify Vision[4]

- Have you yielded yourself fully enough to God?
- Have you asked God to unveil his vision for your life, or are

you asking him to bless a plan that you've already come up with? We must come to God with empty hands and an open heart and ask, "What is your vision for my life?"

- Have you fasted?
- Have you prayed?
- Have you been quiet and waited on God in solitude?
- Have you cleaned up sinful patterns in your life?
- Have you weeded out the distractions and ambient noise that would keep you from hearing what God is trying to say to you?
- Have you read avidly?
- Have you traveled widely?
- Have you visited a variety of ministries around the world?
- Have you exposed yourself to the kaleidoscope of visions that God has given to others so that you can be inspired by the variety of options?
- If not, get out there! See what God is doing!

Questions from Andy Stanley[5]

1. Do we have a transferable mission or vision statement?

   - Do our members and attendees know why we exist?
   - By what standard do we measure our success as a church... really?
   - Which of these three drive the majority of our decisions: reaching people, keeping people, or paying the bills?

2. What have we fallen in love with that's not as effective as it used to be?

   - What do we love doing that's not really working?
   - What's off limits for discussion?
   - Do we have any "old couches" that need to be thrown out?

3. Where are we manufacturing energy?

   - What are we promoting that we secretly wish we didn't have to attend?
   - What would we love to quit doing but continue to do because we fear the consequences of change?
   - What are we doing programmatically that we would never dream of inviting a friend to attend?

4. If we all got kicked off the staff and the board, and an outside group (a group of leaders who were fearlessly committed to the mission of this church) took our place, what changes would they introduce?

   - What's the first thing they would do?
   - Who would they replace?
   - What would they refuse to fund?

5. What do we measure?

   - Is there a natural relationship between what we measure and our mission?
   - Are there things we should be measuring that would give us a more accurate read of how well we are accomplishing our mission?
   - What are we afraid to measure?

6. What do we celebrate?

   - Is there a natural relationship between what we celebrate and our mission?
   - Are there things we should be celebrating that would help reinforce our mission?
   - Do we celebrate anything that reinforces a behavior that shouldn't be reinforced?

7. If our church suddenly ceased to exist, would our community miss us? If so, why? What value do we bring to our community? How do people outside our church view our church?

NOTES

Chapter 1

1. "calibrate," Dictionary.com, http://www.dictionary.com/browse/calibrate.

2. Andrew S. Grove, *Only the Paranoid Survive: How to Exploit the Crisis Points That Challenge Every Company* (New York: The Crown Publishing Group, 1999), Kindle edition.

3. Andy Stanley, Deep & Wide: *Creating Churches Unchurched People Love to Attend* (Grand Rapids, MI: Zondervan, 2016), Kindle edition, 303.

4. Bill Hybels, *Courageous Leadership* (Grand Rapids: Zondervan, 2002), Kindle edition, 37.

5. Malcolm Gladwell, *The Tipping Point: How Little Things Can Make a Big Difference* (New York, NY: Hachette Book Group, 2002), Kindle edition, 9.

6. Gladwell, *Tipping Point,* 12.

Chapter 2

7. I am borrowing this term "mission drift" from Peter Greer and Chris Horst in their book *Mission Drift: The Unspoken Crisis Facing Leaders, Charities, and Churches.*

8. Peter Greer and Chris Horst, *Mission Drift: The Unspoken Crisis Facing Leaders, Charities, and Churches* (Bloomington, MN: Bethany House Publishers, 2014), Kindle edition, 19.

9. Harold Fickett, "Interview with Reggie McNeal, Author of Missional Renaissance," The High Calling, February 15, 2010, http://www.thehighcalling.org/leadership/interview-reggie-mcneal-author-imissional-renaissancei#.U81pM6gwIc0.

10. Rainer, *Autopsy*.

11. Acts 2:41, 2:47, 5:14, 6:1, 6:7, 11:24, 12:24, 13:49, 16:5, 19:20

12. Numbers 1:2

13. Dave Ferguson, *Keeping Score* (2014), Kindle edition, 347–349.

14. Ferguson, *Keeping Score* (2014), 475-477

Chapter 3

15. Mark DeVine and Darrin Patrick, *Replant: How a Dying Church Can Grow Again* (David C. Cook, 2014), Kindle edition.

16. Alexandra Wolfe, "Howard Schultz: *What Next, Starbucks?*" The Wall Street Journal, September 27, 2013, http://online.wsj.com/news/articles/SB10001424052702304213904579093583249134984.

17. John P. Kotter, *Leading Change, With a New Preface by the Author* (Boston, MA: Harvard Business Review Press, 2012), Kindle edition, 14.

18. Kim S. Cameron and Robert E. Quinn, *Diagnosing and Changing Organizational Culture: Based on the Competing Values Framework* (San Francisco, CA: Wiley, 2011), Kindle edition.

19.   Gordon MacDonald, *Who Stole My Church? What to Do When the Church You Love Tries to Enter the 21st Century* (Nashville: Thomas Nelson, 2008), Kindle edition.

20.   MacDonald, *Who Stole My Church?*, 84.

21.   Ibid.

22.   Joseph Grenny, David Maxfield, Ron McMillan, Kerry Patterson, and Al Switzler, Influencer: *The New Science of Leading Change,* Second Edition (McGraw-Hill Education, 2013), Kindle Edition, 295.23.

23.   relaunch," Dictionary.com, accessed September 1, 2014, http://dictionary.reference.com/browse/relaunch.

24.   "Planes Utilize Most Fuel During Takeoff," Worldwatch Institute, accessed July 10, 2014, http://www.worldwatch.org/planes-utilize-most-fuel-during-takeoff.

25.   Peter F. Drucker, *Managing the Non-Profit Organization: Principles and Practices,* (HarperCollins, 1990), Kindle edition, 14.

26.   Drucker, *Managing the Non-Profit*, 59.27.

27.   Grenny et al., *Influencer,* 19.

28.   Ibid., 18.

Chapter 4

29.   Samuel R. Chand, *Cracking Your Church's Culture Code: Seven Keys to Unleashing Vision and Inspiration,* Jossey-Bass Leadership Network Series (Wiley), Kindle edition.

30.   Grenny et al., *Influencer,* 295.

31.   "Charles 'Tremendous' Jones Motivational Quotes," Al Argo & Argo Global, http://www inspirational-motivational-speakers comCharlesTremendousJonesQuotes.html.

32. Larry Osborne, *Mission Creep: The Five Subtle Shifts That Sabotage Evangelism & Discipleship* (Exponential Resources, 2014), Kindle edition.

33. Jim Collins, *Good to Great: Why Some Companies Make the Leap...And Others Don't* (HarperCollins, 2001), Kindle edition.

Chapter 5

34. Drucker, *Managing the Non-Profit.*

35. F. Scott Fitzgerald, "The Crack-Up," *Esquire,* originally published 1936, republished February 26, 2008, http://www.esquire.com/news-politics/a4310/the-crack-up/.

36. Jim Collins and Jerry I. Porras, *Built to Last: Successful Habits of Visionary Companies,* Harper Business Essentials (HarperCollins, 2002), Kindle edition.

37. One way to think of this is to consider the difference between mission and vision. Mission refers to the core purpose of a group or organization, the bedrock realities that guide and anchor it and that do not change. The Christian mission, for example, is built around the Great Commission, which never changes, anywhere in time or anywhere on the planet. It always remains the same, whether in France or Ghana or in 2016 or 1932. A church's vision for its own particular ministry, however, almost certainly changes through the years as its community changes and grows. Suppose a church got planted in a rural area, but twenty years later, found itself in a more suburban environment. Would it try to reach commuting business people in exactly the same way as it tried to reach long-time farmers? Probably not. The vision changes, but not the mission.

38. Stanley, *Deep & Wide,* 284.

39. James M. Kouzes and Barry Z. Posner, *The Leadership Challenge: How to Make Extraordinary Things Happen in Organizations,* J-B Leadership Challenge: Kouzes/Posner (San Francisco, CA: Jossey-Bass, 2012), Kindle edition, 49.

40. DeVine and Patrick, *Replant.*

41. Ibid.

42. For what it is worth, the 1896 historic house I talked about in my prologue is the house I moved from the church property June 1, 1993 and totally remodeled.

43. Bill George, *Discover Your True North* (Hoboken, NJ: John Wiley & Sons, 2015), Kindle edition.

Chapter 6

44. Sean Covey, Jim Huling, and Chris McChesney, *The 4 Disciplines of Execution: Achieving Your Wildly Important Goals* (New York, NY: Free Press, 2012), Kindle edition, 27.

45. Grenny et al., *Influencer,* 6.

46. Ibid., 291.

47. Covey, Huling, and McChesney, *4 Disciplines,* 32.

48. Larry Osborne, *Innovation's Dirty Little Secret: Why Serial Innovators Succeed Where Others Fail,* Leadership Network Innovation Series (Grand Rapids, MI: Zondervan, 2013), Kindle edition.

49. Grenny et al., *Influencer,* 62.

50. Covey, McChesney, and Huling, *4 Disciplines,* 41.

Chapter 7

51. R. Frost and T. Hartl, "A Cognitive-Behavioral Model of Compulsive Hoarding," Behavior Research and Therapy 34, no. 4 (1996): 341–350.

Chapter 8

52. Edgar H. Schein, *Organizational Culture and Leadership,* The Jossey-Bass Business & Management Series (San Francisco, CA: Jossey-Bass, 2010), Kindle edition, 3.

53. Chand, *Culture Code.*

54. Kouzes and Posner, *Leadership Challenge,* 79.

55. Chand, *Culture Code.*

56. Schein, *Organizational Culture and Leadership,* 93.

57. Ibid., 94.

58. Ibid., 94.

59. Bill Hybels, *Courageous Leadership* (Grand Rapids: Zondervan, 2002), Kindle edition, 81.

Chapter 9

60. K. E. Weick, "Small Wins: Redefining the Scale of Social Problems," *American Psychologist 39,* no. 1 (1984): 43. Karl attributes the concept of small wins to author Tom Peters, who wrote about it in his doctoral dissertation at Stanford University. For a related treatment of this topic, see P. Sims, *Little Bets: How Breakthrough Ideas Emerge from Small Discoveries* (New York: Free Press, 2011), 141–152.

61. Donald L. Anderson, *Organization Development: The Process of Leading Organizational Change* (SAGE Publications), Kindle edition, 197.

62. Kotter, *Leading Change,* 123.

63. Josh Hunt, *Change Your Church or Die* (Pulpit Press), Kindle, 14.

64. Kouzes and Posner, *Leadership Challenge,* 91.

Chapter 10

65. *Stanley, Deep & Wide,* 270.

66. Ibid., 270-271.

67. Kouzes and Posner, *Leadership Challenge,* 18.

68. Kotter, *Leading Change,* 71.

69. "vision," Oxford Dictionaries, http://www.oxforddictionaries.com/us/definition/american_english/vision.

70. Kotter, *Leading Change,* 71.

71. Kouzes and Posner, *Leadership Challenge,* 143-144.

72. Ibid., 18.

73. Kotter, *Leading Change,* 9.

74. Kouzes and Posner, *Leadership Challenge,* 37.

75. Dave Ferguson and Jon Ferguson, *Exponential: How to Accomplish the Jesus Mission,* Exponential Series (Grand Rapids, MI: Zondervan, 2010), Kindle edition.

76. Bill Hybels, *Courageous Leadership* (Grand Rapids: Zondervan, 2002), Kindle edition, 31.

Chapter 11

77. DeVine and Patrick, *Replant.*

78. Osborne, *Innovation's Dirty Little Secret.*

79. Ferguson and Ferguson, *Exponential*.

80. Osborne, *Innovation's Dirty Little Secret*.

81. "Famous Motivation Quote," Motivation for Dreamers, http://www.motivation-for-dreamers.com/famous-motivation-quote.html.

82. Colleen Barrett, Ken Blanchard, Helio Fred Garcia, Jon Huntsman, Fred Kiel, and Doug Lennick, *Building Success with Business Ethics: Advice from Business Leaders*, Collection (Upper Saddle River, NJ: Pearson Education, 2013), Kindle edition.

83. Frank Lewis Dyer; Martin, *Edison, His Life and Inventions* Thomas Commerford (2012-05-17). *Edison, His Life and Inventions* (p. 127). Kindle Edition.

84. Anthony Wing Kosner, "Jeff Bezos on How to Change Your Mind," Forbes.com, October 19, 2012, http://www.forbes.com/sites/anthonykosner/2012/10/19/jeff-bezos-on-people-who-are-right-a-lot-vs-wrong-a-lot-has-he-got-it-right/.

Chapter 12

85. Larry Osborne, *Sticky Teams: Keeping Your Leadership Team and Staff on the Same Page* (Grand Rapids, MI: Zondervan, 2010), Kindle Edition, 96.

86. Covey, Huling, and McChesney, 4 Disciplines, 13.

Chapter 13

87. Masaaki Imai, Gemba *Kaizen: A Commonsense Approach to a Continuous Improvement Strategy,* Second Edition (McGraw-Hill Education, 2012), Kindle edition.

88. Imai, *Gemba Kaizen*.

89. Collins, *Social Sectors*.

Chapter 14

90. Dallas Willard, *Renovation of the Heart: Putting on the Character of Christ with Bonus Content* (Colorado Springs: Navpress, 2002), Kindle edition, 13.

91. Willard, *Renovation of the Heart,* 13.

92. Ibid., 14.

93. M. Robert Mulholland Jr., *The Deeper Journey: The Spirituality of Discovering Your True Self,* (Downers Grove, IL: International Varsity Press, 2006), Kindle edition.

94. Mulholland Jr., *The Deeper Journey.*

95. Ibid.

96. Ibid.

97. Ibid.

98. Ibid.

99. Wayne Cordeiro, *Leading on Empty: Refilling Your Tank and Renewing Your Passion* (Minneapolis, MN: Bethany House, 2009), Kindle edition, 14.

100. Cordeiro, *Leading on Empty,* 21.

101. Ibid, 26.

102. Paroxysmal nocturnal hemoglobinuria (PNH) is a rare, chronic, debilitating disorder that most frequently presents in early adulthood and is usually continuous throughout the life of the patient.

103. I am only scratching the surface on how the principle of recalibration impacts us in very personal areas. Truth be known, there are other critical areas of our lives that need to be recalibrated at some point, or we will slowly and steadily stagnate as people. Perhaps this is seed for my next book! (Yes, this is a cliffhanger!)

287

Acknowledgments

I am indebted to countless men and women for the creation of this book. My heart overflows with gratitude for all who have provided me with their invaluable time and insight.

My elders and board members at New Life Church continually demonstrated their support for this book, especially through their incredible encouragement and prayer over these past twelve years. New Life Church has been the launch pad for many of the recalibration principles and practices described in this book.

Don Hoffman, one of my elders and board members, has been involved with New Life for forty-one years and has served as elder for each of the four pastors. His contributions to this book, reading and offering insight, immeasurably improved the book's quality.

My own pastor and spiritual father, *Dr. Rick Ross,* taught me how to lead significant cultural change in an established church. I watched with great admiration as Pastor Ross led a historical church into transformational change. His example provided me with a baseline for this project.

Dr. Mel Ming has been a significant influencer for me, starting me down this road of helping established churches to find their full Kingdom impact. His encouragement, insights, and consistent challenges to become a lifelong learner have been valuable beyond words.

Dr. Alan Johnson, my mentor and friend, encouraged me five years ago to think through the principles that have influenced the growth and Kingdom impact of New Life Church. God used his words as a catalyst for this project.

The insights of a great friend of mine, *Brian Jenkins,* have proven invaluable. He spent time helping with the manuscript and asking the tough questions. He has done this with both grace and fortitude.

Jason Miles, bestselling author of numerous business books and a good friend, has provided insights and overwhelming encouragement every step of the way in writing this book.

Dr. Steve Halliday, my editor and publishing consultant, helped me to craft many of the concepts and principles outlined in this book. His insights and encouragement were instrumental to the completion of this work.

I offer my heartfelt appreciation to the seven pastors who were the first to relaunch their churches using the Recalibrate principles and practices: *Andrew Murch, Darrel Johnson, David Brakke, Jeff Duchemin, Mike Acker, Scott Harris,* and *Stan Russell.*

The Assemblies of God Theological Seminary (AGTS) president, *Dr. Byron Klaus, and the entire AGTS Doctor of Ministry team* have been instrumental in the development of this book. They stretched me and built in me critical systems that required that I prove my concepts beyond practice and embed my conclusions in rigorous academic study.

Finally, for my wife of twenty-seven years, *Jana Jones,* I am constantly and eternally grateful. Many times I felt overwhelmed, wondering if I could make this book a reality. Jana never doubted it for a moment, encouraging me every step of the way. Her undying love, support, and commitment to my personal growth and well-being is unequaled. I will love her forever.

About

THE RECALIBRATE GROUP

The Recalibrate Group was founded in 2014 by Dr. Troy H. Jones. Recalibrate is an organization of pastors and leaders committed to recalibrating the 350,000 churches in North America. The Recalibrate Group offers:

- Recalibrate Seminars
- Recalibrate Coaching
- Recalibrate Resources
- Church Consulting
- Speaking and Training

For more information, visit us at www.recalibrategroup.com

RECALIBRATE

Made in the USA
Middletown, DE
23 October 2017